EDUCATION
and a
Woman's Life

Conference Steering Committee

Appointed by the American Council on Education

GRACE M. HENDERSON, Dean, College of Home Economics, Pennsylvania State University; *Chairman*

MRS. MARGARET CULKIN BANNING, Author; Former Chairman, Commission on the Education of Women of the American Council on Education

OLIVER C. CARMICHAEL, Consultant, The Fund for the Advancement of Education and The Ford Foundation

CATHERINE B. CLEARY, Vice-President, First Wisconsin Trust Company

CHARLES S. DAVIS, President, Winthrop College

MRS. LOIS D. IRISH, Assistant Director, College Scholarship Service, College Entrance Examination Board

PAUL A. MILLER, President, West Virginia University

CATHERINE J. ROBBINS, President, Pasadena City College

Conference Staff

From the University of Minnesota

MRS. ELIZABETH L. CLESS, Codirector of the Minnesota Plan for Continuing Education of Women; Assistant to the Dean for Liberal Arts Programs, General Extension Division; *Conference Director*

FRED E. BERGER, Director, Center for Continuation Study

MRS. VERA SCHLETZER, Coordinator and Codirector of the Minnesota Plan for Continuing Education of Women; *Administrative Assistant for the Conference*

BEVERLY SINNIGER, *Administrative Assistant for the Conference*

MRS. KAY BISCHEL, *Receptionist*

MRS. LOUISE ROFF, *Secretary*

EDUCATION

and a
Woman's Life

Proceedings of the Itasca
Conference on the Continuing
Education of Women
Itasca State Park, Minnesota

Edited by
Lawrence E. Dennis

AMERICAN COUNCIL ON EDUCATION · *Washington, D.C.*

© 1963 BY AMERICAN COUNCIL ON EDUCATION
1785 MASSACHUSETTS AVENUE, N.W., WASHINGTON 36, D.C.
Library of Congress Catalog Number 63-22466

Printed in the United States of America

Foreword

MEANWHILE, back in the kitchen is another person. She does not work. Life requires of her merely that she cook, launder, and dust, shop, diaper, and scrub. She manages an establishment of more or less unruly personnel, only one of whom did she interview prior to accepting. She is purchasing agent, finance officer, processor of raw materials, and public relations counsel. But she is called "just a housewife." It is currently fashionable to mull over the role of the woman; to try to reconcile her biological nature with social freedom; to analyze her strengths and man's weaknesses; and to resolve the problems of her discontent via whatever means can be imagined—more education, less education, psycho-therapy, a new type childhood for girls. How a woman interprets her work reflects how she defines herself as a woman within the limits of social boundaries.

from an essay on "The Meanings of Work"
by Sidney J. Levy
published by the
Center for the Study of Liberal Education
for Adults

Preface

ON SEPTEMBER 6–8, 1962, the American Council on Education, with assistance from the Carnegie Corporation of New York and the University of Minnesota, sponsored a conference on the Continuing Education of Women at Itasca State Park, Minnesota. This publication is a report of that conference.

Plans for the Itasca Conference were developed under the aegis of the Council's Commission on the Education of Women, the members of which rendered a distinguished national service through their combined and unstinting efforts to focus public attention on the serious need for more educated women in the United States. During the period of its work, 1960–62, the commission was guided by the beliefs stated in its policy statement of April 1960, *The Span of a Woman's Life and Learning*, one of the most widely distributed statements ever published by the Council.

Special acknowledgment for the success of the Itasca Conference should go to the Conference Steering Committee—Grace M. Henderson, chairman, Margaret Culkin Banning, Oliver C. Carmichael, Catherine B. Cleary, Charles S. Davis, Lois D. Irish, Paul A. Miller, and Catherine J. Robbins—and to the conference staff so ably headed by Mrs. Elizabeth L. Cless. The Council is also grateful to the University of Minnesota as the host institution, the staff of the remarkable facilities at Itasca State Park, and the officers of the Carnegie Corporation, whose financial assistance made the conference possible.

Editorial responsibility in preparing the report of the conference proceedings was shared by the editor with Mrs. Cless and Beverly Sinniger of the University of Minnesota staff, and with Mrs. Mary Iversen of the Council staff, to all of whom we shall be everlastingly indebted.

LAWRENCE E. DENNIS
Editor

Contents

List of Tables

A Woman Is a Woman
Is a Woman . . .

O. Meredith Wilson
President, University of Minnesota

THE UNIVERSITY OF MINNESOTA is honored to be host to this conference, and it is with more than formality that I express our warm welcome to you. The fact that we are at Lake Itasca is, in a way, symbolic. Here are the headwaters of the Mississippi River. This is Longfellow's "land where the father of waters seizes the hills in his hands and carries them down to the ocean deep in its sands to bury the scattered bones of the mammoth." Only big things should arise in such a setting; we expect this conference to develop ideas of great significance and proportion.

It is to education, the means by which civilization is achieved, that this conference is directed. Education is not something to be dispensed to all people in the same quantity or in the same way. If you would deal with it properly, you must first determine who is to be affected. Thus, if you deal with the education of women, as you propose to do at this conference, it is important first to know what woman is. From this flows the title of my address: "A Woman Is a Woman Is a Woman . . ." It is a title that emerged from my lack of understanding of women and of Gertrude Stein.

Having chosen the title for this address, I became concerned with how little I knew of Miss Stein and her writings and proceeded to read them. As a result of my reading, I am probably better informed on Miss Stein than I am on women's education. At the outset I assumed that the words "A Woman Is a Woman Is a Woman" were chance alliteration, and that the proper mood with which to express them was one of perplexity. I discovered, however, that this particular form of expression appears at least a half dozen times in widely separated parts of Miss Stein's writ-

1

ings. In the poem "Sacred Emily," it appears as a simple, hard line, "A rose is a rose is a rose." In "An Elucidation," it takes the form, "To suppose to suppose to suppose,/Suppose that a rose is a rose is a rose." Several references are made to it in *The Autobiography of Alice B. Toklas*. There I discovered that not only was it so much a part of Gertrude Stein's literature that it became her hallmark, but that it appeared on her linen, her stationery, and even on a ring that she wore. It was, in fact, her way of expressing what to her was a major premise about literature.

In one paragraph in which she tried to explain literature, Miss Stein made clear that the thing she discovered, or invented, for literature was the principle of insistence. Some called it repetition, but to her there could be no such thing as repetition. And so you must read "A rose is a rose is a rose" or "A woman is a woman is a woman" as a series of continuing, differing, and accentuating affirmations. I would like to read a fascinating quotation from her writings. It worried me a little to use it as a basis for this talk, but the quotation charmed me. She wrote, "When I said 'A rose is a rose is a rose' and then later made that into a ring and made poetry, what did I do? I caressed, completely caressed and addressed a noun." A man needs to be careful in moving on from that rendering to the discussion of women. Yet it does help provide an estimate of the importance and the affection with which we approach the problem.

Another quotation pertinent to my choice of title is: "Civilization began with a rose; a rose is a rose is a rose is a rose." I would like to change this to read: "Civilization began with a woman; a woman is a woman is a woman is a woman."

At this point you might ask whether in our discussions of the education of women our concern should be for the plight of women or for the needs of society. Personally, I am not concerned with the plight of women; not as the central problem in the present discussions. I believe our concern should be for the needs of society; the need for society to discover better ways to draw from women the capacities for culture and for civilization.

The first part of our discussion should be merely a rephrasing of what would be said in any discussion on education. Here my language could be almost exactly what it would be if I were talking to members of the legislature of the State of Minnesota, appealing for funds to carry on the work of the University of Minnesota, or precisely the same language that John Neumaier would use appearing before the same legislature for funds for Moorhead State College.

Western civilization cannot be explained properly without understanding the forces of formal education that operate in its midst. In the United States, almost nothing which we now know could continue, much less improve, without education. I once tried to determine the economic consequences of education. I had a professor of economics—a man for whom I had great admiration —provide me with the record of growth in per-hour production of American labor in the period between 1900 and the year of my request, which was 1956. According to his statistics, there had been a 3.3 percent increase per annum in the per-hour productivity of an American laborer during that period. If the 3.3 percent were considered as cumulative, then a typical American laborer engaged in productive enterprise in 1956 would have been 375 percent more efficient than his grandfather had been fifty years earlier.

How do you explain this increase in productivity? No one is willing to allege that man in 1956 had more muscles than man had fifty years earlier. No one is ready to allege better conditioning, for most of us have at some time participated in conversations in which adults were complaining of the softness of their children. A part of the increase might be attributed to additional capital investment, but this alone does not explain it. In the end it is apparent that approximately 50 percent of the annual gain in productivity resulted not from additional capital investment but from additional intellectual investment. The burden of life had shifted from man's back to man's mind.

Many changes have taken place in higher education in the past fifty years. A significant change relates to the number of women enrolled in higher education. In 1920 there were almost as many women attending colleges and universities in this country as there were men. Today the ratio in total enrollment is approximately three men to two women. Why this is so, I can offer only an armchair reflection.

In 1920 education was largely available to, and used by, a

relatively urban, fairly well-to-do segment of American society. The university was, in a way, a socially oriented organization. Going to college had economic consequences, but it was not yet a fundamental and central economic factor in life. Most of those enrolled in colleges and universities were from families who did not have to debate the question, "Which will we educate if we cannot educate all?" In today's society it is for the bread-winner, or the potential breadwinner, that a college education assumes major importance.

Related to this is another body of statistics of concern to admissions officers in institutions of higher learning. Half of the upper 25 percent of students graduating from high school do not go on to college. Most of these are women. In high school a girl is more conventional, more disposed to conform, more mature, and more ready to meet the norms required by the central office than are the boys. She is less subject to disciplinary actions and more likely to do her homework. As a result a dis-proportionate number of girls are in the upper 25 percent of high school graduates. The fact that our society has not thought it important that these girls go on to college helps explain why so large a part of those in the upper 25 percent of high school graduating classes fail to do so.

Beyond this concern for the failure of a high percentage of girls to continue their education beyond high school, there is a national concern—and certainly a Minnesota concern—with those who do go on to college and earn their degrees but then are with-drawn from productive society. It is at this point that I get troubled. I would like to see women educated, and their educated selves employed to the best advantage of society. But there are many schools of thought about what should happen in the educa-tion of women.

I read for this conference a series of papers written primarily for people in home economics, hoping to get a better under-standing of this aspect of women's education. One of the first things that struck me was a comment which I doubt I could find in any other writings on education. The author described two schools of thought about general education and said that home economists believe in the second. I have never before met so solid a phalanx among any group of educators. It was a sweeping proposition and implied that if I really got to the heart of women I might find a body of conformists who would agree on an educational proposition that would tear asunder every other group of scholars with whom I am acquainted. Perhaps my failure to recognize the possibility of this uniformity among women is but a symptom of my inability to understand women and their needs. That may be true, for when asked, "What should be included in the education of women?"—whether speaking of general education or education with a professional objective—I am disturbed by the disposition of many to separate mankind intellectually into two sexes.

A distinguished American, the late William Faulkner, had a view of what women should know. Faulkner observed that a woman needed to know how to ride a horse, how to tell the truth, and how to make out a check. These are important, I imagine, but I have never encouraged my wife to ride a horse after learning that she could do it better than I. I have never felt that I needed to urge her to tell the truth, and I learned early that she is quite competent at writing checks. Not only does she write checks but she is so busy with the management of our household that I find the statistics of the Department of Labor peculiarly lacking in insight when they describe women as unemployed unless they have a formal employer. What a distorted view of the facts of American life! These statistics also distort the problem you must deal with in a conference on the continuing education of women, for they obscure the objectives with which you must be concerned as you talk about the constructive roles, the contributing roles, the useful roles for which women should be prepared.

I must acknowledge, however, that when Mrs. Wilson and I sit down to talk with our children about curriculum we approach our sons' problems differently from the way we approach our daughters' problems.

When we talk about curriculum with our sons—one of them now graduated and one not quite ready to enter college—there is an immediacy relating to vocational or professional objectives that does not exist when we talk with two of our daughters who are presently in college. When our daughters—one a sophomore and one a senior—ask us for advice, they receive counsel that is soft rather than hard in its orientation to vocational life. We do not eschew the idea of a vocation, and when they ask "Should we prepare for something?" we never say no. When questioned, however, about what courses they should take next year, we are almost certain to talk about civilizing and enlightening subjects. We are likely to make compromises with what we think are the instruments of wisdom only when we talk with our sons. While we urge our boys to gain the capacity for reflection and thought, there is always the overriding consciousness that they will need to be employable, for their own good and for the good of their families.

This provides a hint of why the people at the University of Minnesota established the Minnesota Plan. Certainly it is the reason that becomes persuasive to me when I hear its rationale explained. The Minnesota Plan does not begin with the assumption that you should invent special courses for women, even though some may be specially drawn up in the process. It begins, rather, with the idea that a university such as the University of Minnesota has tremendous resources. Given these resources, what is needed is guidance so that the individual may make optimum progress toward her particular career. The program, therefore, has become largely one of advice and guidance. It attempts to be forehanded for the generation fortunate enough to be entering college now, and it also attempts to repair the faults of an earlier generation. For the latter—those who would like either to restore rusty talents to modern use or to complete work previously set aside because they became creators in a different sense—the program provides a foyer for re-entry into the university.

As a conservative, starchy product of a masculine society, who has been modified by a happy life with attractive women, I feel that the sexes are essentially equal and that we should emphasize the common needs and attributes of both when dealing with the problem of educating adults. We are all preachers of reason. Together we should seek a capacity for conversation that will provide an abiding interest on an intellectual level in each household. We all should have some appreciation of the rich tradition which Western society has made possible to us and at the same time a full awareness of the tremendous challenges with which the non-Western world confronts us. To achieve this appreciation and familiarity requires not separateness, but togetherness in the business of intellectual inquiry.

I am persuaded that a woman's voice and a woman's view, where it is different, is an important modification of any masculine conversation. I am equally persuaded that a group of women talking with ever so great animation about papers on international organization or economics or about a historical novel with deep philosophical overtones, such as *War and Peace,* will be better informed if they have an occasional irascible male mind affecting their otherwise idyllic conversations. In the long run, male and female will have to understand life together if there is to be complete appreciation of it.

The place, then, for modifying programs for the education of women is neither in the nature of the materials nor of their content; it is in recognizing that there is a tentativeness about women's commitments to intellectual life during the time they are twenty to twenty-five years old. This tentativeness becomes actual detachment for a period following marriage. The need is for counseling and guidance in the period prior to this time of tentativeness and detachment that will make more certain a later return to the world of inquiry and academic life.

When we speak of man as the creature of reason, we are speaking of mankind. H. G. Wells tells the story of Benham who was troubled during most of his life with morbid dreams of meeting a fierce man-eating tiger in the jungle. He found himself at length attached to a British forestry company on the edge of a jungle in India. Unable to sleep one night, he rose from his cot and was drawn almost hypnotically down a lonely trace into the jungle where he met in reality the dream that had been troubling him for most of his life. Confronted with the tiger, he spoke these words, "I am man, the thought of the world." The tiger flinched and Benham, almost inarticulately repeated: "I am man, the thought of the world." With that the beast slunk off into the wilderness.

If we are anything, we are the thought of the world. If we have any contribution to make, it is intellectual. If there is any persisting inspiration toward mastering thought, or preventing the waste of our potential for thought, it is kept alive and nurtured primarily by our mothers and our wives. It is for this reason that I particularly like to reword part of Gertrude Stein's writings to read, "Civilization began with woman; a woman is a woman is a woman is a woman."

Education and a Woman's Life

Karem J. Monsour
Psychiatrist and Psychoanalyst
Pasadena, California

IN DISCUSSING THE LIFE of women and the educational process, a man ought to step gingerly, since there may be a hint of bias, no matter how objective he tries to be. With this admonition firmly in mind, I would like to present briefly a few thoughts on women and education as they occur to the mind of a psychoanalyst.

It no longer seems necessary to champion the cause of women's education. The current task seems more to understand the life of women, how they adapt to the educational process, what sorts of consequences may result, and what information is available from every source with which to plan and implement further progress in this field.

Grotjahn[1] has remarked that a woman's life is in the family, and that the family is a projection of the woman's unconscious into the outer world. Formation of this unconscious image of a family group is the result of psychosexual developmental processes in the human female. Each stage of development has characteristic emotional patterns which are determined by the life-tasks of that stage. Erikson[2] calls these stages "circumscribed crises of inner-growth which are aggravated by discernible tensions in the sufferers' social condition." One of the discernible tensions in the social condition is the educational ritual. Yet, there are unique aspects of female life that resist influence by culture, society, *or* education. These special features, firmly embedded in the woman's unconscious mind, exert their motivating power on her

[1] Martin Grotjahn, *Psychoanalysis and the Family Neurosis* (New York: W. W. Norton & Co., 1960), p. 94.

[2] ERIK H. ERIKSON, Introduction, *Emotional Problems of the Student*, Graham B. Blaine, Jr., and Charles C. McArthur (New York: Appleton-Century-Crofts, 1961), p. xiv.

behavioral patterns throughout childhood, adolescence, and adulthood. They give rise to the curious realism of the woman and her optimistic, self-reliant nature which represent a kind of resigned acceptance. For instance, one might hear a woman say, "It isn't that you've ruined the best years of my life, it's just that you've spoiled my day!"

The beginning formation of these unique womanly qualities begins with the earliest maternalizing influences in the little girl of two and a half years. This process continues throughout childhood, puberty, and adolescence. A firm identity as a prospective wife and mother is ordinarily well established by the time the girl attains the age of eighteen to twenty.

For this reason, college years are not a satisfactory psychosocial moratorium[3] for women in the same way that they are for men. Women are psychologically prepared to embark on their life-task sooner than men. A four-year college moratorium cannot realistically be expected to detain the young woman in her anxious hopes for marriage and a family. The college environment should be an excellent and approved place to find a husband. Yet, current idealized concepts of higher education often seem incompatible with this primary goal in a woman's life.

Dr. Mary Bunting has noted in women a decline in intellectual interests shortly after finishing college, which is reminiscent of the previous decline in scholarship in the pubertal girl. The reason for this occurrence is that the young college-graduate mother is preoccupied with making use of her body and her capacities in the role of motherhood. Intellectual interests are shunted aside. Specific unconscious orientations direct her concern toward the realities of life and away from the mysteries of the mind.

Assuming, for the moment, that the woman is moderately successful in her motherhood venture, she will have gained an interval of stability in her life, a sense of personal fulfillment, and a quieting of her unconscious demands. She gives up some awareness of the larger world around her in the act of giving her attention to the small world she has created. Cessation of child-

[3] Erik H. Erikson, "The Problems of Ego Identity," *Journal of the American Psychoanalytic Association,* IV (1956), 56.

bearing around the age of thirty, however, limits her reprieve. It is a cruel blow to the woman's unconscious, since interrupting the flow of babies forces her to face a dilemma for which she has no naturally endowed solution. This state of affairs has produced a common clinical syndrome, which one might call the "early thirties crisis." It is characterized by a painful level of tension appearing in various forms of anxiety and depression. There is a recapitulation of many tendencies in the pubertal period such as phobic reactions and sexualized fantasies of promiscuity. Psychosomatic disturbances such as migraine, colitis, ulcer, and menstrual irregularities occur. A solution may be found in club work, volunteer efforts, getting a job, or plain social frenzy.

In Erikson's term, some solutions are generative, others self-destructive. Alcoholism is one of the latter. An excerpt from the conversation of a thirty-two year old woman with three children conveys the nature of her distress and her attempted solution. She speaks: "Most girls go to college with the idea of getting married. A good education seems secondary. Actually, in my freshman year I *thought* I was out to get an education. In my second year, I blossomed a bit and began my search. But I didn't consciously feel I went there [college] to get a husband, yet I somehow felt the idea was to get married by graduation, at *least*. I'm sure that now I don't feel my husband is really superior to me, but I wish I had some concrete evidence of my education. If I could only make myself want to be a teacher, which seems to be about the only avenue open, then I'd feel I could contribute something myself. Why am I always wanting something more? Because I have no *final* goal, I guess, no final aspirations. I had given up before I came here. Why else would I spend my time drinking, looking for oblivion everywhere I could? I felt I was trying to escape from myself." This particular woman had graduated first in her high school class and finished two years of college when marriage interrupted her education. She has now renewed her academic interests in an indirect way by going to work as a secretary to the head of a university philosophy department.

Of course, the educational community is not responsible for the dilemma of many women such as the one quoted above. There are developmental processes in the woman herself which drive her toward the "early thirties crisis," regardless of the educational exposure. Binger[4] describes the young college women he encounters as sensitive, idealistic, and resilient. They uniformly become depressed some time in their college career, but they recover with proper and kindly care. However, after the childbearing period, the woman's unconscious resources for other role choices are less available and much less flexible than during adolescence and early college life.

From these remarks, one concludes that women face a new dimension of the identity problem in the postchildbearing years. Increased emphasis on socialness has made a larger task of midmarriage than it was formerly. Enlarged educational opportunities should assist the woman in this new life task. "A [woman's] soul is an expensive thing to maintain," writes George Bernard Shaw. "It requires special conditions under which to love."

Part of the inertia in activating new educational programs is due to cultural tradition regarding prescribed male and female roles. Cultural traditions, however, have their roots in collective unconscious motives aimed at preserving fundamental relationships which subserve the basic reproductive function. Out of this unconscious matrix emerges a paradoxical resistance in women to any change in the social order. Their resistance is due to a haunting fear of being left alone and empty. This fear persists in the deepest unconscious recesses. It gives rise in women to a silent sanction of many destructive forces around them. In the educational field, too, women seem to cooperate in their own subjugation. Yet, promising signs, such as this conference, appear to show that present generations of educated women have become aware of their folly.

Hopefully, the woman's capacity for creating human life in the family world may be rechannelled into the capacity for infusing humanistic life into the social world. Dr. Albert Szent-Gyorgyi, in analyzing the primitive cave man mentality with which we are trying to run the world, writes ". . . then we have

[4] Carl L. A. Binger, "Emotional Disturbances among College Women," *Emotional Problems of the Student*, Graham B. Blaine, Jr., and Charles C. McArthur, p. 172.

to look for a group which cares and has votes too. There is such a group . . . women, especially mothers. Women have more common sense then men; they have found out that high-energy radiation damages children and refuse to swallow whatever we tell them about permissible limits. They simply want none of it. I have the keenest hopes about peace groups composed of women."[5]

There are other resistances which account for inertia in comprehensive programs for women's education. Male dominance at high levels of educational administrative authority resist, with anxious caution, revision of the educational scheme originally designed by and for men. Such anxiousness in men is deeply felt, albeit disavowed consciously. It is questionable whether there is an immediate remedy for this situation. The traditional liberalism in educational circles, however, may gradually attenuate this resistance factor.

Yet, there is a resistance factor peculiar to the educational process itself. From the psychological viewpoint, education is as much a mind-training process as it is a learning one. Any mind-training method, however benignly used, has suppressing effects on mental life. Since education has a culture-transmitting function, and since adults educate children, it is difficult to escape the conclusion that education is to some extent always partisan. This function of education is subject to easy abuse and is used for fostering conformity to established rules. Educators who sincerely attempt to establish educational innovations such as are necessary to encourage women in their intellectual efforts will find themselves frustrated by inherent resistances in the very educational processes they are trying to use. At the very least, they should attempt to maintain a continuing awareness of this inescapable problem.

A primary effect of the educational process is to raise the level of symbolic mental function. This effect accounts for a relative increase in the prevalence of neurosis which can be thought of as a disturbance in symbolic processes. Education tends to replace (intuitive psychological) understanding with the logical, rational thinking prevalent in Western culture. Although the absolute

[5] Albert Szent-Gyorgyi, "Persistence of the Caveman," *Saturday Review*, July 7, 1962, p. 34.

incidence of mental and emotional disorder is not affected, the kinds of disorders change toward the neurotic, psychologically manifested varieties. Increasing intellectual awareness in women of this change accounts in part for their greater tendency to make use of psychotherapeutic methods.

There is a possible hazard for the future in the current enthusiasm for women's education. To paraphrase a statement of Grotjahn's regarding education by the use of humor, one might say that extensive education of women has not yet been tried in earnest. It would encourage irreverence and lead to a spirit of democracy in the next generation to an extent for which we are not yet prepared.

A certain amount of generalization is unavoidable when the terms men and women are used in any discussion. The unique character of the individual woman may go unnoticed. For this individual women, a paraphrase of Thoreau's words about man is pertinent. "If a woman does not keep pace with her companions, perhaps it is because she hears a different drummer. Let her step to the music which she hears, however measured or far away."

REMARKS IN ELABORATION OF WORKING PAPER

DR. MONSOUR: I want to start out by saying a few things about women and their nature as I understand them. I can describe a few characteristics that many of you may be aware of and that might prove of some general background interest. For instance, women are more narcissistic creatures than men. They are more involved in themselves and their person. They are more self-sufficient people. Their need to be loved is greater than their need to love. What they do is more an extension of their own person than a part of some separate being. For this reason women convey to their activities and to those around them more a part of themselves than men do. They put themselves into their life. Men take on projects; women give themselves to their projects.

The sexual attitude in women is less defensive than it is in men. A friend of mine was going on a hike with a group of young men and women, and they saw a nudist colony down below. He was a middle-aged man and, thinking he would have a little fun, he said, "Let's all go down and see what they are doing down there." The other men promptly scattered in the opposite direction, but the women said, "Yes, let's go right down!" The girls did not seem worried about what they were going to encounter and about the fact that, of course, they would have to, in Rome, do as the Romans do. Women are canny about this attitude. They do not reveal that they really know what sex is all about. One girl, who was being paid some attention by a man, said, "Well, all I could do was blush and look embarrassed." She recognized his intention but tried to help the fellow out by giving him the idea that he was being very clever, but all along she knew what he was up to. She explained to me, "My eyes are very misleading. Men think I'm thinking wild, lovely thoughts when really I'm making out the grocery list." Women seem to have this capacity for detaching themselves. Sex doesn't seem to be a life and death matter to them. I think their attitude toward education is somewhat similar, and I'm going to explore that a little bit later.

There is a tendency toward a kind of inaneness in women, perhaps empty-headedness is a better word, which is very deceptive. A girl said to me, "So President Kennedy has established a commission on women—how delightful—how funny—I wish I knew what it meant." She didn't really think there needed to be a committee on the status of women, and I think she felt that women could pretty well take care of themselves. I am going to challenge that a little bit and see what comes of it. Women are naturally intuitive, and they often don't need formal education. They claim not to understand men, but they simply are not telling us all they know. They probably know a great deal more about us than we want to know or than they are willing to admit. I have a feeling that in educational circles, when women are in charge of things, they more or less tolerate the supervision by men because they feel that they will get their way in the end anyway; they are simply biding their time.

Perhaps the most important facet of women that I want to bring out is that a woman cannot be understood outside the family context. The family image—the family idea—must have originated with women. I'm sure they created husbands; men would never have gone to that much trouble. The family image comes from their unconscious, and they project it into the world around them and, lo and behold, the world becomes what their unconscious is. And one of these things is the family. This family image which they project is not something they have learned from their own family. This family image is probably an inherent, built-in, unconscious characteristic of a woman which starts at a very early age before she really knows what a family is all about. It must start at least at the age of two to two and a half and is a product of the inevitable psychosexual development in a woman's life. Now, I won't go into a lot of technical detail about that except to say that the characteristics of unconscious development in women probably lead to the formation of this unconscious structure which they then project and in which context they probably have to conduct their lives or make some kind of suitable substitute that will provide gratification or expression of this unconscious force.

The woman's identity is that of a mother. There seems to be no escaping that for her. That does not mean that a woman has to become an actual biologic mother. There is a persistent necessity for expression of this characteristic, and women would not survive very well without some expression of this deep and probably unalterable characteristic in their nature. Apparently, women don't need to know a whole lot to fulfill this function. I asked a woman what she thought women should know, and she replied that a woman needs to know how to cook, clean house, and to read so that she can look up things in Dr. Spock and Gesell. Now I think their education should go a little bit further than that, but what she defined were some of the basic characteristics. She was expressing this primary factor in a woman's unconscious life.

It is interesting that the major events around which women's lives revolve are all bloody ones. Perhaps I should not use that word, but being a doctor, blood holds no fear for me. I mention this to point out that women surmount a great deal of violence in their lives—that is, violent experiences that involve actual bloody events—and this makes a great impression on their unconscious development. I mention these few items, which belong to psychodynamic theory, primarily to form a basis for some assertions I want to make about characteristics of women that have to be taken into account in education.

In the family image of the women, she is the mother, and the man is always and forever a son. He can never escape this identity. A man's task is to learn things; a woman's is to train. The woman's main course in her family and in her personal life is to mature and grow. A man's main course is to learn, gather more information, perform. A woman's education really is primarily a part of family growth and maturation. I doubt that a woman's growth can occur in isolation.

At certain times in their lives women are not fully or easily educated. As a matter of fact, during certain periods in their lives they are highly resistant to education. In the early adolescent ages, girls are very difficult to educate, and sometimes they almost refuse to learn. This is the time when, if any of you have a daughter, you will find her coming home claiming that she is having trouble with the teacher because the teacher cannot understand why she is being so stupid, whereas formerly she was a very bright girl. This may last just a few years. When women are in love they are practically impossible to educate. Incidentally, women in love are also very difficult to analyze, which is a hazard we analysts face. They cannot be educated during that time, at least not as profitably as at other times. Women are not very easily educated when they are having a baby; that has been our experience both in psychotherapy and educational ventures. Freud, too, said that women were lost to education and psychoanalysis when they were in love and when they were having a baby. Not only that, he had a rather pessimistic attitude about education in general, as well as about the education of women. He thought that the results were always going to be unsatisfactory. I suspect that there will always be some unsatisfactory results no matter how hard you try, and this is especially true with regard to the education of women. One must be particularly careful, then, to try at the right times.

I am discussing the typical course of a woman's life. There are other courses a woman's life could take, which we would discuss in another way, but let us take this instance: in the postchildbearing years a woman comes up against the difficult problem of a cessation of the opportunities for gratification of her unconscious forces. This creates a degree of tension, which gives rise to a certain critical age in women. This may occur anywhere from the late twenties to the middle thirties and sometimes later on, depending upon the characteristics of the woman. This critical time, then, is a vital matter to educators, since it represents the most opportune time to get hold of women and do something to remedy their condition. The manifestations of tension and crisis at this time are numerous. Some of these expressions are satisfactory, some are frustrating, and some are pathologic. A woman in her postchildbearing years probably feels a real force for independence. She wants, in a sense, to separate herself to some extent from the family, because the family no longer offers her the chance to continue to generate and to create. She searches for some fulfillment in her own work. Hopefully, educational measures will provide here an important outlet for the tension which will in turn obviate the need for other symptomatic formations, namely, the somatic and psychological illnesses.

The self-fulfillment of women, therefore, has its opportunities for greatest fulfillment at this particular time. It can be done in a number of ways, all of which embody some symbolic expression of the mothering function. We will not go into the numerous ways that this force can be transferred to other endeavors and still symbolically express the primary force. This transfer may dilute the force to some extent but also may enhance it with certain characteristics which will give rise to creative expression in an important cultural or educational way. Whether or not this occurs in a woman will depend not only on her basic character structure, but also upon the opportunities available to her and how they are presented to her. This is an important aspect of your interest in educational programs.

As a psychiatrist I should be confining my remarks to women, but I am going to say a few things about education. Education from the psychological view is perhaps not so much a matter of accumulating information or gathering knowledge, but rather it represents a mind-training process. None of us knows exactly how education began, but it is possible that in the evolution of culture, education did not necessarily begin as a method of accumulating information. It may have begun as a method of grouping people together in some kind of conforming arrangement where they were able to live together. The education ritual is like many other initiation rites and religious rituals that tend to initiate the person into the context of the group within which they function. This education, then, becomes a process of training the mind, rather than storing information within the mind. The person involved will change his way of mental function so that he operates on a different level of symbolic thought, and it will also lend different characteristics to his character structure. Consequently we find that educating people may change them from happy people to neurotics, to give an extreme example, where they are in more conflict than if they had remained allegedly innocent and naïve. Education, therefore, has some hazards from the psychological standpoint in what it does to the person as a person. In women, educational interests may be, and I say this with some temerity, more of a hobby than a life and death matter. Women have a vital interest other than education. Their vital interest is not necessarily education, and education often may be more a matter of doing something in their spare time. One woman said to me, "After all, what is education? It's just a part of everyday life; finding out something that you didn't know the day before." A man would never say anything like that. Education is for him a matter of covering a great deal of material, acquiring important skills, getting a degree. A woman takes a more lighthearted view of education, and this is more realistic for her. We cannot underestimate the fact that women may not channel all their interests and motivations into their education efforts as a man would.

There is some resistance—as a matter of fact, considerable resistance—to educating women, and the resistance comes from a number of sources, at least in the psychological view. One of these sources is the educational structure itself. Every group, no matter what its composition, tends to become more complex in its organization. The increase in organization requires more conformity and more structure and additional hierarchy, and soon you have resistance to change; thus a new orthodoxy is created from a revolutionary beginning. Education is no exception to this process and will resist change simply because it is a bulky structure by itself and has its own vested interest. Men resist the change in educational structure. They have a paternalistic attitude, and they speak with soft tongues to the girls and say, "Yes, we think you girls really have a good project going there, but keep it small. Don't let it get too big." Because if one really starts educating women, it might get bigger than the university and then produce a change in status which men would resist much more openly the more they were challenged. Men do not have to be too resistant right now, because they have the upper hand. They can afford to be kind and good-natured and pleasant about the whole thing, and in addition, they do it with good intentions and good will. They are not being consciously vindictive about it.

But the most important resistance to the education of women is from women themselves. They simply have built-in resistances to changing the order of things. Their resistance often is not apparent. They are for change and progress. They want to change things; they are militant, they are aggressive. This insistence on being forceful about the matter in many instances, in my view, is an expression of their unwillingness really to change; in fact, they are overcoming resistance in themselves by a compensatory increase in aggressive activity. I think by this that many times they arouse more antagonism than friendship, and this is not an effective way to bring about the change they want. It is necessary for them to recognize that they have internal factors in themselves that do not want to change the way they are or the way things are, and that to overcome this by being militant and aggressive may be defeating their own ends. It is true that integration of women has not yet taken place. They have been politically and economically enfranchised but have not been integrated as far as the sociological view is concerned, and this situation needs to be remedied. I do not think that women can look to the country to make use of their resources. To paraphrase President Kennedy, "Wait not for your country to avail itself of you, but force yourselves to avail yourselves to your country." This may take a little more doing than simply waiting around for recognition to come. Of course, we men want you to do it in a very feminine, charming, and kindly fashion, and please leave us intact when you finish.

DISCUSSION

Moderator: Mr. Louis T. Benezet (President, Colorado College; President-elect, Claremont Graduate School and University Center) : I will violate the moderator procedure to this extent only and suggest that what Dr. Monsour has reillustrated in his general statement is one of three views of women, at least of her education. The first view would be that there is no essential difference between men and women that would have any significance for education at all. The second view is that there is a difference in women which is, however, thrust upon her by the social pattern of man's existence; these difficulties that she labors under—most of which have been thrust upon her by men, as Dr. Monsour has suggested—must be dealt with and surmounted if women's full potentials are to be used. The third view is that woman by her own biology is a different creature. Because of a basic biological difference, her whole attitude and response to education is and will remain different and unique and will affect any kind of educational experience that she enters, with the result that the education itself must be patterned with this basic difference in mind. This is what you would expect the psychiatric view to be. I am quite aware that it is not accepted by many people, and with that open invitation for you to challenge Dr. Monsour, who wants to start?

Mr. Joseph W. Cohen (Director, Inter-University Committee on the Superior Student) : I wish you would clear up a little your views on education, especially if you are talking about institutional education when you say, for example, a woman becomes uneducable at certain times. Are you talking about the educational process in and of itself or are you talking about the unsuitablility for institutional education?

DR. MONSOUR: No, I am talking about the educational process, by itself; at least that is what I intended to say.

MRS. VIOLA HYMES (President, National Council of Jewish Women): When you say that a woman is uneducable at these particular times in her life, are you not really saying that *people* are uneducable at times in their lives when they are extremely disturbed or concerned emotionally? I observed that when my sons were in love and in a state of insecurity they were not particularly educable.

DR. MONSOUR: I will have to resist that challenge and say that I stand my ground, and I will try to tell you why. I think that a man is still approachable while he is in love because his primary interest is not the matter of love. His primary interest is in his drive to accomplish something, and this is always in the back of his mind in his love affair; although his love affair may seem tempestuous at times, it is not really as wholehearted an interest with him as it is with the girl. With the woman, being in love is an entirely different state than with the man; it takes over her whole unconscious interest. In other words, her total person—unconscious person—is going in this direction, and no room is left over for someone else to sneak in with a little bit of education.

MR. JOHN S. NEUMAIER (President, Moorhead State College): My view would be that you should think of women as people rather than women as women, because what do we men know of women? I would like to have the conference be concerned with women as people, and we might find under certain circumstances that women act very much like them.

You exaggerate observability, for instance, and immediately jump to the conclusion that these are innate differences and not a difference of degree. I would point out the difficulty in assessing to what extent the difference might actually be the female part of the species and to what extent the differences might be socially, economically, culturally, and historically determined. I think that this is very, very difficult to assess and that we ought to step gingerly in drawing conclusions about the causes.

DR. MONSOUR: My opinion, then, is diametrically opposed to yours. I believe that the difference is an important one, that it has to be emphasized and cannot be blurred away, and that the cultural context has almost no influence upon these factors that I mentioned. The kernel of the questions is, "What is it about a woman's nature that one should take into account in planning an education program?" You are all aware of the social context in which we live, which is why the educational system automatically takes this into account in its structure. I do not think that the cultural, social, or economic context has anything to do with the points I mentioned. I think they are inherent in a woman, and they will be there regardless of whether she lives in Afghanistan or Madagascar or in Itasca State Park and will have to be viewed that way. I do not think that I am making too much of this point. I want to come back to the question "Can we do something by educational processes and experience that will lessen this difficulty?" I am inclined to believe that if this is to be done it has to start at a very early age. In other words, you have to start in the primary grades and envision an educational circumstance that will take these features into account. I do not think you can start at a late age and encourage women to be more attracted to education and that this will then supersede, or at least will deter, them in their interest. Not that one should not strive to light the fire of educational interest in women. After all, that's what we are all trying to do. But I don't think one should be too sanguine about that.

MRS. FELICE SCHWARTZ (Founder and first Executive Director, National Scholarship Service and Fund for Negro Students): I very much agree that the nature of woman is different from the nature of man. I think that in addition to this variation we must recognize that the *life* of a woman is different from that of a man; that is, if she does want to raise a family, it seems to me terribly important that she be realistic about the fact that her educational goals cannot be as comprehensive as a man's. A woman often feels guilty about the fact that she is not amortizing the cost of her education, but if she leaves home, she also feels guilty that she is not doing her job as a mother. It seems to me that we must address ourselves to being more realistic about what we expect from her. If we want her to contribute thirty years of service in order to justify her education, then we don't want her to be a woman; we want her to be a man. I think we would be doing a great service both to the woman and to society if we became more realistic in our goals and said, in the case of a woman who is interested in medicine but who also wants to be a woman, we will invest money to educate her, but we won't expect thirty years of service from her. We will be satisfied if she spends fifteen years being a mother, and we will not expect more than fifteen years of service in her profession. Let her relax and enjoy both and probably contribute much more in each stage because she is not guilt ridden in either one.

DR. MONSOUR: That brings up the question of goals—the plans of the program. What are the goals of education of women? There has been a considerable discussion in the literature on that point, and I think it is a very difficult area in which to talk. First of all, who is going to evaluate what these goals should be? You are talking about what contribution we should expect the women to make—fifteen years or thirty years of service. This presupposes a value system—what is valuable, what should be accomplished, and what women should do. Now I think this is a very difficult area. One is expressing some personal bias when he talks about what should be accomplished from the standpoint of the cultural and societal needs and what women should contribute to them. I still prefer to look at it from the standpoint of the woman herself: What does she want to do? Who cares what society needs her for or what should be expected of her?

MR. BENEZET: Are there not a number of women whose processes of sublimation are so deep and so successful that their actual contributions to life and their orientation to life can be successfully judged by that sublimation rather than the fact that certain ego impulses—id impulses—are repressed? Their whole contribution to society must be evaluated by that successful sublimation.

DR. MONSOUR: You are taking us into a very difficult conceptual field of sublimation. All I wish to say about that is that the effects of what we call sublimation can be highly satisfactory in the accomplishments of any person, man or woman. What I thought you were going to say when you started was: Can't women express themselves in sublimated ways other than having a family and having babies? Of course, they can. However, the way they express themselves, if analyzed and traced very carefully—that is if they are successful or live with some kind of peace with their efforts—always includes some elements of the primitive unconscious forces that I mentioned. For instance, every woman who has accomplished anything really important has been wedded to some great cause or principle and is in a sense married to her determined view of what she wants to do.

MRS. VIRGINIA SENDERS (Member of the Education Committee of the President's Commission on the Status of Women): I don't understand all of what has been written about sublimation and repression and regression, so I am not going to talk about those things. It seems to me that the practical question with far-reaching consequences that you have raised both in your paper and in your statements this morning is that there are certain periods in a woman's life when she is uneducable. Essentially, you assert that during the very years that she is in college, a woman is least amenable to the educational process. Now you go further and assert that this is biologically determined, and when you are asked what your evidence is, being a psychiatrist and a psychoanalyst, you resort to case histories. Now, I am not attacking you or your discipline personally, but we have all had case histories. The consequences of your assertion are that the whole pattern of education should be rethought from the point of view of the timing of it; this seems to me to be practical, but I think what the later discussion points out is that we don't have enough evidence on it. This is an easily researched topic. Enough women are in love in the colleges today to provide us with some good evidence, and presumably, an equal number of college men are in love, too, although not necessarily with the same women. There are pregnant women, and though there are not pregnant men, we could use men with other crises in their lives as a control group in this research project.

I have one other comment to make. I know the case history of a young woman in love whose learning was disrupted. She is one of our Minnesota Plan women, and I feel pretty proud of her. I feel that she is somebody we saved in time. This girl had strong professional ambitions for most of her life. She wasn't a very attractive girl, and other factors in her background precluded normal dating. I don't think it ever occurred to her that she might get married. She was going to be a mathematician, and she was heading in that direction when she fell in love. Then everything went to pieces. Her grades went zoom, and she herself kind of went zoom. She had always—in her concept of herself— seen herself in the role of a professional mathematician with a Ph.D. Suddenly there she was in love with a nice, young naval ensign, and the future looked so completely different from anything she had seen in the past for herself that she could hardly reconcile herself to the change. She was referred to our counselor because of the drop in her grades and because she was thinking of dropping out of school in her junior year. Well, our counselor neither examined her unconscious nor traced back her ego development. He simply said, "Look. There are a few facts about women's lives that you ought to know." I don't mean this was entirely didactic, but they did tackle some of the immediate practical questions: Can you get married and keep a small apartment and still be a student? Can you go to school on a full-time basis? Can you do it on a part-time basis? When is a good time to start having children? How much life is left over after the children are grown? How many children are you going to have? After some counseling sessions of this very practical and down-to-earth sort, the girl picked up where she had left off, completed the incompletes on her record, and graduated with the same kind of record she had been making all along. Incidentally, she is now married, has one baby, and is continuing to progress in a slower way toward her goal of becoming a first-class mathematician. If it is possible to do that sort of thing that simply, then I don't think we need to say that because of biological predispositions and unconscious motives, we can't educate women of college age.

DR. MONSOUR: Women of the college are educable. All I am saying is that you have to know how to do it. And you had better take into account the facts that need to be taken into account in order to do it successfully. I think that girls should be started in school much earlier than boys. I would be in favor of starting girls in school at four and boys at six or something of that kind. I could talk to you about a number of ideas concerning what I think should be done about the educational programs of boys and girls. I think they should be planned differently. I don't want to sound entirely negative about my attitude about educating women. I think the education of women is probably one of the major forces for social change in this country and will continue to be and that continued large numbers of educated women will bring about social change all by themselves.

Mr. Thomas Carroll (President, George Washington University) : I would like to ask your opinion about the desirability of coeducation versus separation by the sexes.

Dr. Monsour: I don't think that girls have to be in separate classes. I think that four-year-old girls could be in the same class with six-year-old boys and be at their level of educational ability. I do think that there are certain times in educational life where coeducation is not as desirable as at other times. I think that junior high school is a particularly difficult time for coeducation and only compounds the injury rather than salves the wounds that occur at that time. I also feel that certain college ages possibly may be better educated separately than together. The social problems involved for girls make them somewhat frantic during their college years, and they become frantic to the point where they get more involved in the problems of love, marriage, and childbearing than they might do under less-pressured circumstances. And the coeducational exposure at that time might be somewhat difficult for them, depending upon the girl. On the other hand who is going to keep an eighteen-year-old girl back?

Mr. Carl Grip (Dean of Men, Temple University): Dr. Monsour, I get a completely different impression from your discussion this morning from that I got from reading your paper. It seems to me that in the paper you took a position that gave a greater importance to culture in influencing the pattern of the feminine life. Today you have given us the impression of a fairly rigid life structure for the women. Let me make this specific by referring to an illustration you used in the paper. You pointed out that when the flow of babies is interrupted there is a crisis in the feminine identity, and I certainly think this is true. Let me use as another illustration the experience that the woman has when she sends her first child off to nursery school. This would precipitate the same kind of an identity pattern or problem.

We found that the woman who had the greatest difficulty in parting with her child tended to be the person who was already neurotic; in other words, turning the child over to the nursery school was not the cause of her problem, but the difficulty was the consequence of a pre-existing identity problem. If this is true—and this seemed to be applicable to the later stage when the woman ceases to have children and begins to turn her attention to other activities—isn't there room for a much more permissive attitude toward precisely what the patterns are for women, rather than dogmatically predicting a pattern of an entire life that simply revolves around having babies?

DR. MONSOUR: I have gotten myself in a difficult position here. I can see that in attempting to emphasize the major point, I have perhaps sounded much more dogmatic than I wish to sound. I don't want to convey the impression that I am not aware of the cultural and social factors involved in women's status. As to your point that women can find sources of gratification other than this alleged immutable unconscious force, all I wish to say is, of course, they can. The personality formations are obviously unlimited and give rise to various kinds of endeavors that women undertake. The point I wanted to make was that in all these endeavors one finds the kernel of the basic forces that I have tried to emphasize, and that these basic forces have to do with the way in which women learn, the way in which they mature and grow, the way in which their personality structures form, and the way in which they express themselves.

The Milieu of the Educated Woman

C. Easton Rothwell
President, Mills College

Much has been said in recent years about the problems of the woman who wants to gain an education, to amplify it in subsequent periods of her life, and to use it effectively. Imaginative steps have been taken to help women meet these problems. By holding this conference, however, we acknowledge that much more must be done. In part this is because the problems themselves are not standing still. They are growing and changing as an increasing number of women strive to cultivate their talents and to use them more effectively in the work of the world. A major part of our task here is to discover with some certainty the forces in our society that are causing this to happen and to identify the steps that will offer further help to women in the realization of their aspirations.

My subject is the milieu of the educated woman, but I cannot approach it without an awareness that many aspects of what I shall say about women are equally applicable to men. Without wishing to minimize the problems that are peculiar to the educated woman because of her sex, I submit that many of the problems we shall be discussing really involve educating *people* and helping educated *people* serve themselves and society well.

The milieu of the educated woman encompasses her from the moment, as a girl, she undertakes the task of gaining an education. It is the milieu of her life, and it affects her capacity to keep her education alive, to strengthen it. It also determines how often she will be able to use her education and how well she will do so.

Marriage and family formation is without question the most important of all the forces that condition the education of women. This has always been the case. Nonetheless, the trend of the past two decades toward early marriage and the early bearing of reasonably large families derives special significance from the fact that it has coincided with a sharp increase in the number of women enrolled as college undergraduates and graduates. The impact of marriage and family upon the education of women and upon the educated woman is thus increased. Moreover, this is taking place at a time when the optimum use of human resources, both male and female, has become an essential goal of the nation. In consequence, the role of woman is more complicated and more challenging than at any time in this century.

Whereas the effects of the current trend are of great interest and demand the most careful analysis, we must not assume that the trend will continue indefinitely. A glance at the 1920's, and especially at the 1930's, should remind us that social patterns might change markedly if we should experience a little economic belt tightening, a shift in the requirements for personal security, or a change in the mores and social pressures affecting our youth.

One cannot escape the conclusion that early marriage and family formation or the anxieties about them are indeed interrupting the education of women. They are causing women to leave college; they are placing women under psychological pressures that diminish their academic performance; they are exerting some negative influence upon the pursuit of graduate degrees and careers.

The data which support these conclusions must be handled with great care, however, lest they mislead. For example, there is a high national attrition rate among women undergraduates, a rate that is undoubtedly related to early marriage. But there is also a high rate of "fall out" for men, and marriage may have something to do with this too. The statistics on graduate education disclose not only that the number of women who complete the bachelor's degree and thus become eligible for graduate work is just over half the figure for men; they also show that a progressively smaller proportion of women than men attain the master's degree and, ultimately, the doctoral degree. This is somewhat surprising in view of the concern of women graduates to obtain the master's degree as part of the preparation to teach.

In the light of these rather discouraging figures about women's graduate work, it is gratifying to learn from the June issue of *Women's Education* that a large proportion of the recent gradu-

ates of Eastern women's colleges and certain other colleges intend
to start graduate studies in the autumn. The average reported for
the women's colleges was just under 30 percent, whereas at Carleton College, City College of New York, and Brooklyn College the
proportions of women continuing their education were 44 percent, 60 percent, and 62 percent respectively. I might add that the
comparable figure at Mills College this year is 34 percent—higher
than in any previous year.

These ratios are important for two reasons. They indicate a
gain over previous years in the number of women undertaking
graduate work, at least for the master's degree. More important,
they suggest a significant overlap with marriage. I draw this
conclusion from information concerning the marriage rate of
Mills College graduates, which I believe does not differ significantly from the marriage rate of women at other colleges and
universities. Over 40 percent of these young women enter matrimony within one year after graduation, more than 80 percent
before the end of five years. The relatively high overlap between
graduate work and marriage is self-evident on the basis of these
figures. What will be the effects in the long run of this expanding
common ground between matrimony and advanced education remains to be seen. I suspect, however, that if one analyzed the
records of women who did graduate work during the past decade,
while at the same time maintaining a married household, the
findings would be very encouraging.

There are, of course, factors other than marriage and family
formation that interfere with the education of women. Economic
pressure upon the parents is too frequent a cause, especially when
it is aggravated by insufficient financial assistance from the college of the girl's choice. Inadequate work opportunities is another
factor and causes young women to suffer to a greater extent than
do young men. The failure of parents to encourage within a
girl the aspiration to attend college is a familiar factor and is
often linked to the assumption that because a girl will marry
soon, there is less reason to educate her than her brother. So much
has been written about these and other factors, however, that I
need not labor them.

My principal purpose is to consider the elements within our

society that help or hinder the young woman who wishes, after leaving college, to keep her education bright, to deepen it, and to put it to uses that will be socially significant and will at the same time help her realize her potential.

For the able, liberally educated woman, the years during which her children are young, underfoot, and making interminable demands upon her interests and energies are difficult. Yet, if we are to keep the young mother's problem in focus, we cannot isolate it from the realities which are equally pressing on her husband and her single sister who are facing similar frustrations during the same period. These are the years when a young man is serving what amounts to an apprenticeship in a business or profession. The budding executive is checking someone else's accounts with grammar school arithmetic; the developing diplomat is stamping visas. These activities may involve little of their liberal arts education, which they may begin to think of as a useless extravagance. The single woman on bad days during this beginning stage of her career may likewise have doubts about her education and look with envy upon her childbearing classmate's solid, if squalling, evidence of accomplishment.

And yet, if the education has been sound, the mother, her husband, and her single sister will normally come through the difficult years with the durable results of their learning unscathed if not enriched. The lasting outcomes of a genuine education are curiosity, concern, a yearning for self-expression, and the capacity to satisfy these hungers intelligently. We need to know much more about the educational circumstances that produce these qualities. Nevertheless, the number of young couples who remain intellectually alive and vital through the early years of marriage and career is evidence that a good education can last and flower even amidst frustrations. Only when the learning has been superficial, or has not "taken," or when it is thwarted by personality factors, do its effects attenuate during the first years of marriage.

The period in a married woman's life that causes most concern to those of us who wish to see her achieve the maximum realization of her potential is the span of active years that remains after her children are in school. The question most frequently raised is, "How will she employ in fullest measure during those years the education she acquired a decade or more earlier and has managed to supplement formally and informally during her children's youth?" How will she?

I recently raised this question when speaking to a lively group of young mothers five to fifteen years out of a variety of colleges. They had just spent a year analyzing their own reactions to a questionnaire on continuing education and the job potential of the mother whose children are in school. Although these young women may not have been representative of all those in their suburban community, their group did include many emerging leaders. Their husbands were successfully making their way up the ladders of professional or business advancement. Despite their knowledge of the proportion of alumnae mothers who return to work on a part-time or full-time basis when the children are in school, or perhaps because of that knowledge, these young women were almost unanimous and wholly unequivocal in their rejection of any return to work as an alternative to spending their full time as wives and mothers. They were hostile to any insinuation that woman can be a "wasted asset."

I cannot know how typical these young mothers are of others similarly situated throughout the United States. I applaud their aspirations for their families and the intelligent roles they have conceived for themselves within the home and community. Somehow I did not feel that they had "returned to the cave." At the same time I suspected, and I am confident some of them suspected, that the national averages will ultimately catch up with certain of the group. They will seek work as a means of supplementing the family income, probably to help educate their own children in a period when college education becomes ever more expensive. They will seek unpaid outlets for their interests and energies in the PTA, the Red Cross, reading groups, investment clubs, alumnae or alumni associations, the AAUW, and the League of Women Voters. Some indeed are already at work in volunteer activities. This pattern seems to be a normal and widespread one. Is it one which brings maximum self-fulfillment; which makes the fullest and most intelligent use of the young mother's talents?

The self-realization a woman may attain will depend upon

her own aspirations and her will, as well as upon the opportunities available to her. So far as opportunities are concerned, today's college graduate mother lives in a society which provides almost unlimited possibilities for significant and satisfying volunteer activity, a subject to which I shall return later. She also lives at a time when the working role of women is greater than it has ever been in the United States, thanks in large measure to the pioneering enterprise of women who cared enough about certain interesting kinds of work to penetrate the barriers of custom and thus open them to other women.

The working mother is not a rare phenomenon in the United States. She constitutes one-half of all women of working age who are in the labor force. Indeed, almost one-third of all married women are employed, a proportion that it is predicted will increase substantially by 1970. It is a striking commentary upon our society, however, that less than one-sixth of the women who are working have had some college education and only one-eighth of them are professional and technical workers, the largest proportion of these being teachers.

Nonetheless, the college graduate mother returning to work will find herself in numerous company. She will also find certain patterns of opportunity that will shape and limit what she can do. There is an expanding area of significant and reasonably interesting positions—some traditional and some new—into which she will be welcomed. These will include, of course, teaching, nursing, and social work, which have long been regarded as within women's sphere. But there will also be a chance to exercise her judgment and her mathematics in computer technology and programming and, hopefully, in the posing of problems for which computer programming is used. Her capacities for responsibility and for the rendering of decisions will find outlets in an increasing number of high level places in industry and banking, and in legislative and administrative positions at the local, state, and Federal levels. Moreover, she will find a broadening range of opportunities in science and engineering. There will be careers for her in journalism and, to an increasing extent, in dentistry. But she will find less outlet for her talents in other professions—particularly, law and medicine. Even in these, however, there are certain areas of specialization which male practitioners look upon as being suitable for women—juvenile delinquency, for example, and pediatrics.

College alumnae mothers have been accused of drifting into jobs instead of pursuing planned careers when they return to the labor force. This is true in a large number of cases and, in my judgment, is wholly justified. The mothers who avoid the demanding preoccupation of career most frequently do so, not out of a desire to find a softer life, as some writers have implied, but out of the conviction that their primary interest and energies must be devoted to their children until they are older. Some women, to be sure, can manage career and family well, but a much larger number do not possess that capacity or energy. Consequently, they search for the part-time opportunity or for the kind of job that can be done at home. This type of employment is broadening in range, incidentally, as electronics firms and other employers discover that they can tap a rich and reliable working reserve by using these methods. I have been speaking of a deliberate choice of noncareer jobs. There is also, unfortunately, the young mother who would really like to work toward a career, but who is lacking in adequate preparation and even in sufficient comprehension of the requirements of the profession because of the absence of suitable guidance and career planning when she was in high school and college. Sometimes these women strike out to learn a new field when their children are in school. They can take heart from a recent study made at the University of Chicago which concludes that women over forty who did well in high school can actually learn more rapidly and effectively than their younger college classmates.

Actually the mother returning to work behind the shield of her husband's secure salary and position has a much greater opportunity to experiment with employment than do men. She can "try on" jobs to see whether they suit her talents and temperament. She can take the time to refurbish her skills and tarnished knowledge. She can even run the risk of plunging into new fields of learning, because failure will not effect either her economic status or the standing of her family in the community.

Little need be said about volunteer activities except to suggest that they are a much more essential part of the social and political fabric of the United States than of most other countries. They are a very important element in our democratic process. And they offer the college graduate mother a wide range of outlets for her talents that are neither dull nor make-work, but can challenge profoundly her creative and managerial capacities.

Earlier I commented that the self-realization of a woman will depend as much upon her aspirations and her will as upon the opportunities open to her. To aspirations and will, I should, of course, add ability and a sense of direction. Then I should say that the interweaving of these attributes can help a young woman toward satisfying self-realization at any stage in her journey through high school, college, graduate work, marriage, and motherhood, and the ultimate return to rewarding activities outside her home. One can name many women who exemplify the optimum blend of these qualities and who might serve as models for girls and young women at the beginning stages of the long journey. The Margaret Chase Smiths, the Mary Buntings, the Millicent McIntoshes, the Anne Morrow Lindberghs have all made the journey with distinction in their generation. I am sure that every teacher and administrator at this meeting can name women now on their faculties or in their student bodies who are launched in the same direction. The most important question to ask about them and their distinguished predecessors is where the drive and vision and high aspirations came from. In some cases the colleges are the source that kindled these drives, but I suspect that in most instances the source of the kindling must be sought earlier—in the schools and in the family. Indeed, ingredients of the flame, if not the flame itself, may have their origins in the genes.

In this paper on the milieu of the educated woman, I have attempted to describe the forces and factors which affect her as she moves through the several stages of her life. I have not sought to prescribe for the problems she encounters. That task remains for others. I must record my conviction, however, that her life— whether within the family, outside of it, or in some combination of the two—will more likely result in wholesome self-fulfillment and socially significant accomplishment if she is given excellent counseling and challenging fare at both the high school and college levels. This is the fundamental and formative period. Hence I am attracted to the pioneering that is being done in this field. I find especially hopeful the program in continuing education that is in progress at the University of Minnesota and the program instituted this year at Sarah Lawrence College. Although it meets a different purpose, the Radcliffe experiment is badly needed for women who have gained some level of professional competence.

This is perhaps an appropriate place to set forth a conclusion that one cannot avoid reaching as he works through the scattered literature on the educated woman and regards the experiments being carried on in her behalf. There is serious need for pulling this literature together systematically, for deepening and broadening the study, and for extending the experimentation in some rational fashion. Our understanding would be facilitated if we had more detailed information about certain categories of women at various stages in their lives. We need more case studies of women who have either successfully or unsuccessfully sought to combine family and career. And we need analyses of control groups that have not chosen this course. Only thus will we make sufficient headway with the continuing education of women.

Let me add one final note. When we contemplate the continuing education of women, let us think not only of their repreparation for a place in the labor force or in the realm of volunteer activities, but also of continuing education to expand the ranges of knowledge possessed by both the wife and her husband. Together, they must face intelligently the most rapid and drastic period of change the world has known. This is not easy, and it requires systematic preparation. The problem is stated well by Dr. Robert D. Calkins, president of the Brookings Institution:

> In this fast changing world of discovery and innovation, new concepts, new fields of knowledge, political and social revolution, shifting values and changing philosophies, and the flood of daily events, only the most determined can keep their bearings. . . . [It is essential] to discover and to develop more informed leaders and to establish respected places where the most thoughtful people are glad to go for intellectual stimulation and

refreshment, and for a contemplation of the truly great issues of our society. Even a few places of this character and a few men of this character can make an enormous difference in any community.[1]

REMARKS IN ELABORATION
OF WORKING PAPER

MR. ROTHWELL: I am setting aside my original paper for the moment. I am prepared to stand responsible for the things that are in it and prepared to answer questions on any points that I have made, but I should like to devote my comments here to two points. I would like to say something about the nature of the literature that is available on the education of women, and, second, I should like to say a little about the different phases in the process—a lifelong process—of the education of a woman and the problems of the educated woman. I should like to do the second first and then move back to point one.

As I read through the papers, I was much struck by the projects —some of them very imaginative—that are attempting to deal with the problem of the continuing education of the adult woman. I applaud all of these. I think, as I have attempted to indicate, that they are performing a distinctly valuable service. But I hasten to add that, in a sense, we are making up for our deficiencies with these kinds of programs. The real problem of the education of woman and of what happens to her following her education needs to be coped with during the years when she is most impressionable and most educable, and though I find some inconsistency here, most evidence suggests that this period occurs during her elementary school, high school, and college years. Consequently, I should like to emphasize this really creative and formative period.

I suggested in my paper that some qualities that we want in a woman may be there by virtue of the genes that she bears. I am confident that the elements out of which one can kindle the flame in woman that will carry her through many of the vicissi-

[1] From "New Tasks for Our Universities," an address given before the National University Extension Association, Lincoln, Nebraska, April 30, 1962.

tudes of life are there to start with, but there is a great deal that we can do. Having taught in elementary school, junior high school, high school, and graduate school, I am going to draw on this experience in making some observations. It seems to me that if somehow we can achieve the kind of education that Dr. Monsour started to develop for us—an education that is a formation of the mind and a formation of the person—in such a way that interests are aroused and curiosity is whetted, ideas will be implanted which will have great importance in later life. In addition, if we can cultivate some capacity for judgment, some ability to martial large bodies of information, some capacity to examine assumptions with a critical and objective eye, some ability to assess values and to make commitments with respect to values—if these things can be accomplished before a woman becomes involved in raising a family—I am quite convinced that they will carry her through the later periods. They will tend to diminish the problems a woman must confront when she reaches that later, and very educable, age when her children are in school because they will have immunized her and given her the inner resources for coping with the problems that arise when her children are very young.

This, then, is what we mean when we talk about educating women. Instead of the term "continuing education," it seems appropriate to use "sustained education" because what we are undertaking is to do something during this period that can be sustained. It is the self-generating, self-starting mind and creative spirit that we are seeking to evolve.

Another point that I want to make is about aspirations and expectations. During the early, formative period in a young woman's life, we are implanting the aspirations that will guide her educationally not only during her undergraduate years but in the years following graduation. If the pattern of aspirations is sufficiently rich and the level sufficiently high, I would have great confidence in her capacity to overcome some of the normal frustrations that confront her when she has to bear children, rear her family, and keep her husband happy during the difficult early years of their marriage. During the early, formative period we should quite consciously implant within her a pattern of expectations about her own future. Today, as I talk with young women who are graduating, I discover that often the pattern of expectations is cut off with marriage, which is regarded as a terminal thing. The pattern of expectation needs to look beyond marriage with some considerable realism about events that are going to occur. It can be a pattern that will point out to the young woman a whole sequence of alternatives she might explore singly or in combination as a means of successfully meeting the problems of her family, of successfully bringing about her own self-realization, of successfully making an essential contribution to the community and to the culture of which she is a part. I don't think we do these things well enough.

Let me interject at this point the caveat that I attempted to put into my paper and which bears upon some of our discussion. I think that men, too, have frustrations and problems during their early working years. Their problems are of a different kind from those of women but of the same magnitude. What I have suggested about implanting a pattern of educational aspirations—of expectations—in women applies equally to men and would help carry them through that difficult and rocky period.

President Meredith Wilson, in discussing the problem, referred to counseling as one remedy. I am wholeheartedly in accord with this, and I applaud what is being done through the program at Minnesota for the continuing education of women. I don't think, however, that counseling is the complete answer. I would hope that we could experiment with educational programs in elementary school, junior high school, high school, and, certainly, in college which by their tone, or if I may borrow a phrase from the anthropologists, by their style, would tend to make a real contribution toward implanting that kind of education which includes a pattern of expectations and aspirations for young people. I am sure this can be accomplished.

In a recent study of college values, there was considerable emphasis upon the role of the character or style of an institution as a distinctly formative factor. I think this is very important and would suggest that the current emphasis on the study of student cultures or the culture of a whole college community in relation to the academic aspects of the community is a significant move that will open whole new vistas to us not only in the education of women but also in the education of men.

Now let me come to the other topic: the available literature on the education of women. As I read the papers, including my own, I was much struck by the fact that apart from those which describe specific projects, we have, in a sense, a series of concentric circles, and the common area within these concentric circles is very large. I doubt that I have added much that is significantly different from what appears in the other papers. I have written about the education of women for a year, and with the assistance of our dean of students, our librarian, and a lot of other people who assembled material for me, I covered a great deal of the existing literature. There is a basic sameness to it—a covering and recovering of the same ground. One can perceive the growth of certain clichés and the continued repetition of these clichés. I don't mean to be critical because I have participated in the process and have made my own contribution to the perpetuation of clichés. However, if this meeting is to be really significant, we ought to take a fresh look at the directions we can move to expose new areas of knowledge that can be creatively helpful to us. I don't pretend to have more than a few tentative suggestions, but I hope that they will stimulate you.

Let me start with the literature available on the areas of activity open to the mature woman once she wants to re-enter the work force. (Somehow the term "work force" grates, but, nevertheless, that is the technical term.) The Women's Bureau of the Department of Labor has done a superb job of pulling together a tremendous amount of data on this. Some of the more recent developments, however, may not be encompassed in this data. I would like to suggest as one possible area of inquiry—and I should like to see it done in the most scientific and thorough way possible—an examination of the activities open to the mature woman and the trends and changes that are taking place. We must not look at things in the dimension of 1960; we need only to look back, as I've attempted to suggest in my paper, to the 1930's and the 1920's to discover that trends do change and change quite significantly in this whole area. I should like to see a study that would look ahead for a period of ten years. All the colleges

are engaged in making ten-year plans. I should think that those
interested in the education of women might also look ahead
and anticipate changes that may come about in the patterns of
employment and opportunities for women in various fields in the
course of the next decade and also identify those factors that
can be changed or manipulated. With all of this clearly identified,
one would have some basis on which to proceed.

Let me give an example of what I mean. It was assumed a
few years ago that corporations would make contributions to
colleges at a very limited level and in certain distinctive patterns. Along came Frank Abrams of Standard Oil Company of
New Jersey, Walter Paepcke of Container Corporation of
America, and a few other able, public-spirited people. Through
the formation of the Council for Financial Aid to Education,
some of the manipulatable factors were seized upon, and today
there is a generous response from the corporations in America
to the needs of higher education. I don't think this is the best
example, but this is the kind of thing I mean. I believe that the
Commission on the Education of Women has performed a very
important function in the sense that it hung a star in the
sky and said this is something to which we must give attention.
Now I think the time has come to approach the problem of the
education of women in a much more systematic and scientific
manner.

Let me conclude by referring to what we might do at the
student level. I must confess that I've worked in this area only
three years, and there's a great deal of literature of which I am
ignorant. But I don't believe we have a series of studies on the
various types of counseling that would come to grips with the
problems of implanting a pattern of expectations and aspirations
in women and that would demonstrate the pattern of counseling
most effective in a given circumstance. I'm not sure whether we
know that counseling at the University of Minnesota might be an
entirely different kind of phenomenon than counseling at the University of Oregon, at Mills College, at Radcliffe, or at Columbia
University. I'm sure each school has its idiosyncrasies, but we
need detailed evidence of this. We need to know a lot more

about the impact of the campus culture—whether it be the campus of the college, the high school, or the junior high school—upon personality and character formation and the formation of a pattern of aspirations. I'd like to know whether the campus culture is a stronger formative force than what happens in the classroom or the influence of some distinguished and able teacher. Such studies are just beginning. Some of them are included in *American College: A Psychological and Social Interpretation of Higher Learning* by R. Nevitt Sanford,[2] but much additional work is needed.

It seems to me that information from such studies could open up new vistas and bring us closer to solving the problems that confront women today. There is a wonderful opportunity for the women's colleges to conduct such studies, and the coeducational institutions should also participate. They educate many more women than do women's colleges. The problems of educating women are different in the context of coeducation than they are in the context of segregated education, and I could expound a number of hypotheses about the differences. What I should like to get away from is the current impressionistic character of the literature in this field and find something that is harder and more firm upon which we can build. Now I'll stop and accept your questions.

DISCUSSION

MR. BENEZET: Dr. Rothwell agrees with the previous speaker that women are a problem—an educational problem—to other people, mainly men. However, stabilizers can be implanted early in life which help carry women past more difficult periods in their development, but whatever these stabilizers are, whatever the problems with which they deal, we ought to be more systematic and perhaps more total in our attack to filter out the kinds of knowledge that we want for fair and adequate counseling patterns.

[2] John Wiley & Sons, 1962.

MR. ARTHUR HITCHCOCK (Director, American Personnel and Guidance Association) : I think what Dr. Rothwell has said really fits strongly into a pattern rapidly emerging in the whole area of guidance—mainly a quite decided shift in emphasis. It is generally agreed that the junior high school years are the crucial period for guidance and that at this time we should be more concerned in counseling with the emergent patterns of life or styles of living. One of the ideas emerging now is to look into the future in terms of changing patterns of life instead of being confined to the logic of the trends of the past. Past trends no longer can be projected into future patterns of living.

MR. ROTHWELL: I would like to make just one comment about that. Sometimes university faculties do not adapt readily to this kind of administrative readjustment in a field such as guidance. To change the tone of a college or university, the new idea must be diffused among the faculty, so that a consciousness of the change is fairly well spread throughout the institution. This is easier to accomplish in the smaller institution which is less, if you will forgive me, institutionalized.

MRS. RUTH USEEM (Research Consultant, Department of Sociology and Anthropology, Michigan State University) : I think there are many opportunities for the college-educated woman to participate in the programs we are talking about. There is a real opportunity for the college-educated woman to bring the educational advantages that she already has to those sections of our society which are in need—whether that be in professional or volunteer work. I think here women may find some of the roles by which they can adjust to society.

MR. ROTHWELL: It has often occurred to me that even though men hold the front positions and the titles in our voluntary organizations, women frequently do most of the work. The voluntary organization is a very important part of the whole fabric of the American and democratic structure—politically and socially —so this is an important role. In enumerating the chief reasons for seeking to make a woman's education one that will enable her to accomplish what she wants in life, I would put self-fulfillment at the top of the list. The satisfaction of the national need for additional manpower comes below this. When women accomplish the first, the second will come almost automatically.

MRS. HYMES: I was gratified to hear Dr. Rothwell's statement about voluntary organizations. I have spent a lifetime working within a voluntary organization and have perceived in the past decade a downgrade both of voluntary activity and of the value of the organizations. A continuing of this downgrade will have a dire effect upon social development in the future. In what practical ways do you perceive that we might be able to make women recognize and appreciate again that the voluntary organization is a significant institution and is worthy of their participation?

MR. ROTHWELL: In the first place I suppose that courses in government and in the social sciences could give more place in their curriculum to an emphasis upon volunteer organizations. I suppose, too, that in the procedures of guidance some emphasis could be given to them, and some students could be made aware of the role the voluntary organization plays in our society and the role the well-educated woman plays in the organization. By well educated, I mean the woman who knows how to organize and has developed some managerial capacities. Usually such women have had some managerial experience at a lower level through their own extracurricular activities while they were in high school and college. They know how to get things started, how to handle a meeting, how to organize a conference and take care of the practical aspects of it. Voluntary organizations need much more careful exploration than they have recently received. I might add that I talked recently with a physician from San Francisco who told me that he thought participation of women in volunteer organizations was an exploitation of women. He said they are paid nothing, only a part of their capacities are used, and they do not have the sense of concrete personal satisfaction that professional women get. Well, take this as you will, I think something can be said about women having been exploited, but I do not think that exploitation is the norm in volunteer activity.

MR. ERNEST MCMAHON (Dean, University College and the University Extension Division, Rutgers—the State University of New Jersey) : I would like to comment on Mrs. Hymes's question about the downgrading of the volunteer worker. It seems to me that some of the reasons for the downgrading fall within the area of education for correction. One is that we are in a society where many welfare activities have become professionalized, and, unfortunately, the volunteer worker in many instances continues to be an amateur. I believe that if many of the voluntary organizations encouraged continuing education on the part of their participants so that they could equal the professional social worker, for example, some of the stature of the voluntary organizations might be regained. I think that is probably the most important aspect of their problem. Second, we live in a society which almost makes a fetish of organizations, and too many voluntary organizations operate haphazardly. It seems to me that education can contribute in this respect by strengthening the capacities and the organized approach of voluntary organizations.

MR. BENEZET: I would like to ask the speaker whether he is satisfied with the drift the conversation is taking or whether he wants to bring it back to some other point in his own presentation. Would you like to reguide us or carry on with what we have gone into?

MR. ROTHWELL: I think that we could spend a good deal more time discussing the range and the fruitfulness of voluntary activity, but perhaps it might be useful to go back to the earlier problem of where to put major emphasis in the education of women and what steps to take to make this emphasis sustaining—self-sustaining —if I may go back to one of the terms that I used. It seems to me that this is the area of inquiry that we need to look at. I would also like some comment on the need for a systematic investigation conducted experimentally by professionally competent people into the whole range of problems that touch upon the education of women. The results of this investigation could introduce new concepts, new ideas, and new goals into our discussion.

MR. PAUL WARD (President, Sarah Lawrence College): I was struck when reading your paper by the example of the group of young mothers who rejected the idea of returning to work while their children were in school. I wonder whether more recent literature clarifies all that might be involved for other young mothers who might want to work during this period. Would it be possible for them to carry forward responsible parenthood into those hours and days when they are involved in part-time or full-time work? What kinds of problems would be submerged? What kinds of risks would be involved? Would you comment on this?

MR. ROTHWELL: What you are suggesting is something that was raised during our last discussion, namely, that some of the things we do, and perhaps the example I cited in my paper was evidence of this, are culture-bound evidences of our own society. Maybe these young women—most of whom had two or three children— who insisted upon remaining home and following what they felt was their prime responsibility instead of going to work, who in a sense rejected the idea that a married woman with a family ought to go to work, are simply a reflection of something in our society. I suspect that part of the attitude of these women may be due to something that happened that night, however. In reporting the fact that I was going to speak, unfortunately, the newspaper left out the question mark at the end of the title of my talk, which was "Women—A Wasted Asset?" So there was a certain level of hostility in the audience that night. When I spoke, I didn't know about this. Nevertheless, I think the young mothers were quite genuine in insisting that their prime responsibility while their children were growing up and getting into school was in the home. I felt they saw this as a prime responsibility overriding all others, and I'm sure this view is a reflection of our culture. This brings me to another dimension of what I was trying to get at earlier when I suggested we study something about college cultures and the interrelationships between them and intellectual activity. I am quite sure that many aspects of our college and university culture patterns are a reflection of the general culture of the American scene. I think it would be quite interesting to determine by experiment whether it would be possible to change this cultural pattern and whether there would be any essential loss if a change took place. Different cultural patterns prevail at other levels in American society. When we look at the less-privileged classes in this country, for instance, we discover that in many cases children take care of children. The oldest child frequently takes care of the younger children while the mother is out earning part of the livelihood for the family.

MRS. ESTHER WESTERVELT (Department of Guidance and Student Personnel Administration, Teachers' College, Columbia University) : When President Meredith Wilson spoke last night, it occurred to many of us women that being the wife of a university or college president is in itself an occupation, and this can be true of the wife of a rising young executive, too. To make a home for her children and her husband, such a woman probably cannot take even a part-time job. In other words, we have to compare women and look at their total situation. When their children are in school, housework does not take up the whole day for some women, so they turn to volunteer careers or paying careers. But for other women, partly because of their husbands' occupations, this isn't true. How would you help a girl see these possibilities?

MR. ROTHWELL: This is part of what I was talking about when I said we should implant a pattern of expectation in women. It certainly is true that there is a diversity of occupations for women and many different types of women. Some women are seriously interested in having a career, and other women are more interested in the home. Some women have energy in abundance, whereas other women don't have the same energy levels. In other words, we must not make the mistake of generalizing too glibly about a woman's character.

We have a relatively small faculty at Mills. Five members of our faculty have wives with Ph.D.'s, who teach, maintain their homes, and have at least one child. Most of them have more than one child and continue to do the professional work for which they prepared themselves early in their lives. This is one pattern. There is also the pattern of the young women whom I mentioned in my paper who had families of about four children and who said, "We don't want to go to work. Our interest and our attention is, for the moment, right here." Well, I cannot take exception to this because I feel they are doing a good job. And, incidentally, most of them are taking part in a number of volunteer activities, even though they did not talk much about this. Another pattern— and I think my paper indicated my sympathy for this type of woman—is that of the woman who searches for a part-time job because her time and energies are so limited that she cannot handle both a career job and her children as in her heart she feels they should be handled. We might be able to change our culture somewhat, but we have also to change this woman's heart. It is possible to accomplish this change, but I think we should be careful when doing so.

MRS. WESTERVELT: There is one point I want to make, though, Dr. Rothwell. Many women are not too involved in their husbands' occupations and have long hours when they are not with their children. Those of my children who are still at home leave for school at 7:30 in the morning and get home at 3:30 or 4:30 in the afternoon, and I know that this is a common pattern.

MR. ROTHWELL: Many jobs are opening up that can take care of the woman who is in this very situation. My own wife worked part time, and I am sure many men here could say the same of their wives. My wife handled a reasonably responsible professional job during the period of the day when it was possible for her to be away from home and came home when our children got out of school. Some businesses are recognizing that women in this position are a tremendous resource to be tapped for man power for certain types of jobs and are arranging their schedules to suit women who wish to work part time. Now I wouldn't discourage a woman whose aspirations are to move on to full professional attainment and full professional expression, and perhaps we should be more inspiring to those with such desires. But there are women without professional aspirations to whom we can suggest these alternative patterns.

DR. MONSOUR: There are now many different kinds of vocational opportunities and occupational styles, and we need to know more about the life patterns involved. There is, however, a large group of women who are extremely difficult to mobilize, and I find them often in my own work. If I say to a woman in her midthirties: "Why don't you get a job?" She has a very negative response to this. "Why don't you go back to school and take a few courses at the local college?" She isn't interested or she is not able to get herself going. Although many women do not react this way, in my experience an extremely large group of women does. One reason they react this way, I feel, is because of their need to cling to the forces that anchor them to their homes and from which they are unable to escape without considerable guilt, and they develop a general phobic reaction to going out—either to work or to school. Women must recognize and overcome this hazard. They must become conscious of the problem in themselves. This should be accomplished, hopefully, in an educational context during their coeducational training in their earlier years so that they are made aware of this problem.

Needs and Opportunities in Our Society for the Educated Woman

Esther Peterson

Assistant Secretary for Labor Standards and Director of the Women's Bureau, U.S. Department of Labor

THERE IS A GROWING LITERATURE about the needs of educated women. Longer lives, healthier children, advanced technology, mass production and distribution, and a world that has managed to stay at peace affords us a measure of assurance that our women will have more and more leisure during, and especially after, the years of child care. If leisure implies uselessness, it is a sweet coating for a bitter pill. Each of us needs the inner satisfaction of making a continuing contribution, however small, to the society in which we live.

What about the needs of the community for the talents of educated women? There is no shortage of problems to tax the ingenuity and talent of educated women. The recent Ford Foundation *Statement on Policy for the Sixties* identifies among its large problem areas elementary, secondary, and higher education; the strengthening of our democratic institutions; the problems of urban growth; and youth development. Common experience reminds us of the possibilities for improved health services. We lack doctors, nurses, and hospital administrators. With a sharp increase in the numbers of the aging, our health services will be even less adequate. The shortage of scientific personnel in the face of the explosion of scientific knowledge has created a problem of indefinite proportions. This list is not exhaustive; it includes only the obvious "firsts."

And yet we are not coming close to educating all the women and men who have talent. We need better public schools. American children suffer from basic inadequacies in our public education system. More thought and action is needed before every child

—white or Negro—whether from suburb or slum, city or farm, has the chance for full personal development. We will improve the public schools with the help of Federal aid, state aid, foundation programs, and more imaginative use of the educated women in our communities. We need to salvage the child—boy or girl—who leaves school. We need to solve the problem of substandard housing. A Lincoln can emerge from a log cabin, but the overcrowded Spanish-speaking tenements on the New York upper West Side are not likely to produce many like him.

These problems are being attacked from many angles. The President's Committee on Juvenile Delinquency is carrying forward in selected communities a concentrated effort by all agencies—educational, welfare, health, and judicial. It is working toward the development of formulae for community action capable of widespread application. Foundation studies and programs have carried us a long way forward. Many communities are already working on their own problems with their own resources. In all these efforts to broaden the horizons of the community of tomorrow, there is an important place for the talent, imagination, and dedication of the educated woman of today. We need information about the opportunities that exist and how they can be made sufficiently flexible to fit the life pattern of those who are married and have children.

Who are our educated women?

Broadly speaking, we are talking about the women who have a college education, with the realization that not all women who have been to college take advantage of the education offered and many who cannot go to college manage to educate themselves. Educated women are not a small elite, although they are a minority. During the past six years, college enrollments for women have increased proportionately more than for men. As a result, the percentage of women among all college students has moved steadily up from 34.6 percent in 1956 to 37.7 percent in 1961. In 1920 less than one-third of a million women were enrolled in college. In 1960 there were one and one quarter million. We expect enrollments of college women to reach one and three quarter million in 1965 and two and one-third million in 1970.

The rate of growth is more impressive than the actual numbers. From 1920 to 1960 college enrollments of women almost quadrupled. In 1920, 16,642 bachelor's degrees were granted to women. In 1950 there were 104,000. In 1960 the number reached approximately 132,000—an eightfold growth in 40 years. In 1970 the figure is expected to rise to 234,000. Yet, these figures indicate that a significant number of women do not finish college. We need to understand more about the reasons.

Mrs. Mary Bunting has made one suggestion: "Precious little attention has been given to designing educational opportunities to meet the needs of married women. Rather, we have assumed that if she marries early she is not interested in continuing her education. The possibility that the choice could be a question of timing rather than goals has not received serious attention."

The Women's Bureau has just completed a study, *Fifteen Years After College: A Study of the Alumnae of the Class of 1945*, in which 580 alumnae of four colleges told us what we have come to expect to hear about the life pattern and interests of mature, educated women. It is especially noteworthy that the study questionnaire, which asked about marital status, children, employment, interest in work, training, and education, struck a responsive chord—about 85 percent of the 674 alumnae of the four colleges answered the questions.

A majority of these college women from the class of 1945 reported that they felt the need of additional education or training to obtain the type of position they would like. The percentages of women reporting this need was highest, of course, among those not employed at the time of the survey. A majority of the survey alumnae were housewives not working outside of the home. Their greatest interest was in further academic education or university courses. Significant numbers wanted to take courses leading toward teacher certification; a few reported interest in business and commercial courses.

High proportions—that is, from 46 to 63 percent of the participating alumnae from the four colleges—expressed an interest in a paid position for the future. Many graduates were already employed, although the figures ranged from 16 to 45 percent among the four schools. Higher proportions of graduates than nongradu-

TABLE 1: PERCENTAGE DISTRIBUTION OF EMPLOYMENT STATUS AND PLANS
OF ALUMNAE,* CLASS OF 1945, IN FOUR COLLEGES

STATUS	ALUMNAE			GRADUATES			
	Total	Non-gradu-ates	Gradu-ates	A	B	C	D
Total respondents.........	100	100	100	100	100	100	100
Currently employed: total.......	32	25	33	33	36	16	45
Full time.................	19	16	19	19	20	7	30
Part time.................	13	9	14	14	16	9	15
Seeking a position: total........	2	1	2	2	2	1	......
Interested in a future position: total.....................	53	49	53	54	50	63	46
Within 1 year.............	4	9	3	4	2	......	2
About 2 to 5 years..........	15	4	17	21	20	13	8
Perhaps later..............	34	36	33	29	28	50	36
Not interested in a position: total.....................	14	25	12	11	12	20	8

* The term "alumnae" as used in this report refers to all members of the class of 1945, both graduates and nongraduates.

Source: *Fifteen Years After College: A Study of Alumnae of the Class of 1945*, U.S. Department of Labor, Women's Bureau Bulletin 283 (Washington: Government Printing Office, 1963).

ates were employed. (See Table 1.) Of the graduates who had had one or more paying jobs since graduation a majority reported a professional position as their most responsible job. The proportions ranged from 50 to 73 percent of the graduates of the four colleges. But 18 to 34 percent considered that their most responsible position had been clerical in nature.

The undergraduate major of the college graduates affected the nature of the job they had been able to get. There were larger proportions of professional workers among graduates who had majored in a technical or specialized field (nursing, health, chemistry, biological sciences, social work, or physical education) than among those with majors in the liberal arts (foreign languages, English, history, music, or social sciences). Of the nongraduates with some employment history, the proportions reporting professional positions ranged from only 11 percent to 29 percent in the four colleges.

A vast majority of the alumnae who were interested in future employment showed a preference for part-time work, but many of them lamented the scarcity of such opportunities. There was also some interest, particularly among the alumnae who were not employed, in obtaining assistance in choosing a suitable field of work. Though from only four schools, these findings confirm the mature college woman's interest in further learning and active participation in our society.

Aristotle tells us that "learning is an ornament in prosperity, a refuge in adversity, and a provision in old age." Although we live in a time of prosperity, I think that higher education for women is not ornamental; it is necessary for our survival as a free democratic society. From the beginning of our nation, our founding fathers recognized the importance of widespread general education, because they realized that only an educated people can expect to preserve democratic freedom. We recognize this necessity today in offering newly emerging nations our help and encouragement in meeting their own educational problems. Where higher education becomes the rule rather than the exception, this privilege must be shared by women, not only as a matter of simple justice, but because we cannot do without educated women in our homes, in the professions, in business and industry.

Educated women in the home

The significant influence of women in our society is felt first in the home. Women constitute the nucleus of family life. They are the first teachers of our children. For this reason alone, potential mothers should be educated to their highest capacities. It is staggering to think about the resources of knowledge, wisdom, and patience needed to answer truthfully and effectively, hour after hour, and day after day, the steady flow of questions which pours forth from little children. Any teacher can testify to the value of a home where books are read and issues discussed, where there is a love of music and the arts. How much value do we place on this use of education?

Mirra Komarovsky quotes the dilemma of a young mother who, having moved into an apartment with a coal stove, immediately baked a cake to please the children: "My family liked it, so I baked another. They were less enthusiastic, so I baked a pie. My child asked, 'Why don't we have prunes and Jell-o, and what is an amoeba?' "

On the other hand, I am not so sure that we are doing a good job of educating women in home management and in the arts and ways of caring for children. These subjects do not seem to find a place in most educators' curricular discussions, but they are central to a woman's happiness. I suspect that many college-educated women feel uncomfortable in the household routine, not only because we fail to give it the dignity it deserves but because they have never mastered the basic skills that give a sense of pride in the work. Organization of time, so necessary to a successful college career, is even more essential for the well-being of a young mother. Mastery of household skills, wise use of time, and a comfortable attitude toward homemaking can give a woman the extra time she needs for intellectual pleasures when she is housebound.

No woman thinks it is humiliating to go to a driving school when she knows that she will spend a large portion of her time behind a wheel. The need for this training is taken as a matter of course. We need to think more about the kind of education or training needed for homemaking. Should the same education be given to all social and economic groups? Should it be given in school to young people and again later as on-the-job training? There are many techniques for experimentation—educational television; a service (like the agricultural extension service) for urban and suburban women; and "clinics" for health education, nutrition, baby care, and efficient home management.

Educated women in the labor market

We know that a growing number of married women will divide their time between home and a job. We have approximately 24 million working women in our labor force; 13.25 million are married. In fact, a third of all married American women hold jobs. Estimates show that by 1970, two out of every five women of working age will be in the labor force. (See Table 2.) The expected 18 to 20 million wives at work in 1970 may still be in the minority, but their contribution and their problems will have a real impact upon our society.

TABLE 2: PERCENTAGE OF WOMEN IN THE LABOR FORCE,
BY AGE GROUP, 1960 AND 1970

Age Group	1960	1970
18–19	50.9	43.6*
20–24	46.0	45.2*
25–34 †	35.9	38.9
35–44 *	43.2	47.0
45–54	49.4	54.5
55–64	36.8	43.0
65 and over	10.5	12.2

* Decline due to girls' staying in school longer.
† This age group supplies lowest proportion of women workers because of responsibilities at home.

Source: U.S. Department of Labor, Bureau of Labor Statistics.

We can expect married women to return to the work force when family responsibilities permit. It is estimated that by 1970 over half the women in the 45–54 year age group will work, and almost half of those in the 35–44 year group. Three million mature women are expected to enter or re-enter labor force in the 1960's. This trend is not limited to the United States. In a recent Progress Report of the 16th Session of the United Nations Commission on the Status of Women, the United Kingdom, Australia, and other nations reported that increasing percentages of women enter paid employment as soon as their children no longer require their full attention at home.

There is a definite correlation between the amount of education a woman has and the likelihood that she will hold a paid job. A 1959 study showed that half of the women college graduates held jobs, in contrast with two-fifths of the high school graduates and one-third of those who did not go beyond elementary school. These figures remain firm today despite the fact that the probability of a woman's working is shown to decline as her husband's income rises.

We also know that the greatest increase in job opportunities will be found in occupations that require the most education. The rate of growth of the professional and technical group will be twice that of the labor force as a whole—over 40 percent in the next ten years. This will mean a rise from about 7.5 million to 10 million. Specifically, the engineers, scientists, technicians, teachers, and medical and health specialists will increase the most rapidly. (See Tables 3 and 4.)

TABLE 3: ESTIMATED PERCENTAGE CHANGES IN LABOR FORCE REQUIRE-
MENTS, 1960–70, AND EDUCATION OF WORKERS IN 1959, BY OCCUPATION

Occupation	Percent Change, 1960–70	Average Years of School Completed (1959)
Professional and technical.............	41	16.2
Proprietors and managers..............	24	12.4
Clerical and sales.....................	27	12.5
Skilled...............................	24	11.0
Semiskilled...........................	18	9.9
Service...............................	25	9.7
Unskilled.............................	0	8.6

Source: *Occupational Outlook Handbook*, 1961 edition, U.S. Department of Labor, Bureau of Labor Statistics (Washington: Government Printing Office, 1961).

TABLE 4: LABOR FORCE IN PROFESSIONAL AND RELATED
OCCUPATIONAL GROUPS, 1960

Professional and Related Occupational Groups	Number (thousands)
Teaching: total..	*1,775*
Elementary...	1,000
Secondary..	600
College..	175
Scientific and technical: total.............................	*1,860*
Engineers..	850
Technicians and draftsmen...........................	675
Scientists...	335
Health: total...	*1,629*
Nurses...	504
Physicians...	235
Pharmacists..	117
Dentists...	93
Health technicians...................................	330
Others...	350
Other professional and related: total.......................	*2,160*
Accountants..	400
Clergymen..	250
Lawyers..	230
Musicians, music teachers............................	175
Social workers.......................................	105
Others...	1,000

Source: *The Manpower Challenge of the 1960's*, U.S. Department of Labor (Washington: Government Printing Office).

Our growing population and our growing numbers of students through the college level means that our need for teachers is climbing too. Over 200,000 new teachers will be needed each year during the 1960's. (See Table 5.) Almost all elementary school teachers are women, and half of our secondary school teachers are women. A growing demand for teachers comes from qualitative changes in our educational system and changes caused by improvements in teaching methods and in curriculum as well as from population increase.

Research and development work in the areas of atomic power, aerospace, and electronics will create many new jobs for physicists, chemists, engineers, mathematicians, statisticians, and for a vast army of technical assistants. Women now represent about one in seven scientists, less than one percent of the engineers, and a small, but unknown, percentage of the technicians. All of these jobs need specialized training, and many require an intensive academic background. Employers have found women more than adequately able in these jobs, and they are beginning actively to recruit them. Medical and health services are increasing in type and number. How familiar we are with the shortage of doctors and nurses. Important research being done on the causes of disease, the prevention of illness, the effects of radiation, and the

TABLE 5: ESTIMATED NEED FOR TEACHERS IN ELEMENTARY AND SECONDARY SCHOOLS, 1960–69

(In Thousands)

YEAR	ELEMENTARY			SECONDARY		
	Replace-ments	New Positions	Total	Replace-ments	New Positions	Total
1960	88.8	19.0	107.8	52.1	40.0	92.1
1961	90.9	21.0	111.9	56.5	32.0	88.5
1962	93.2	11.0	104.2	60.0	29.0	89.0
1963	94.4	18.0	112.4	63.1	33.0	96.1
1964	96.4	16.0	112.4	66.7	36.0	102.7
1965	98.1	17.0	115.1	70.6	35.0	105.6
1966	100.0	14.0	114.0	74.4	00.0	74.4
1967	101.5	13.0	114.5	74.4	11.0	85.4
1968	102.9	11.0	113.9	75.6	15.0	90.6
1969	104.1	12.0	116.1	77.3	16.0	93.3

Source: U.S. Department of Labor, Bureau of Labor Statistics.

role of nutrition means an expansion in the numbers of trained workers needed.

It is impossible to predict accurately what specific skills and talents will be most needed in the future. Our young people must be prepared for work that does not yet exist and for a life that we can only imagine. The complex nature of jobs will place new emphasis on the quality of work; the demand will be greatest for those with the education and training that fits them to handle such jobs.

Educated women as volunteers

Not all jobs that need doing are in the labor market as such, and the majority of married women do not seek paid employment. For many women the greatest contribution they can make to society and the best outlet for their education and energy is in volunteer work. As income levels rise, many more women will be released for voluntary service.

There are many unmet and urgent needs in the traditional health and welfare area which might be met, at least in part, by the wise use of volunteers. One area which particularly needs exploration is the use of volunteers in growing public agencies. New large areas of need are being recognized which new or existing voluntary agencies might help to meet. There are many fruitful areas for experimentation. Even modest programs which could not be undertaken except by voluntary groups can lead to successful social effort. There are many relatively uncharted areas where experimentation might prove valuable—for example, after-school centers for the cultural enrichment and occupation of teen-agers, community health education and information, counseling and employment services for older persons, training and retraining programs, aids to homemakers and older persons, and care of children. Some volunteer jobs are relatively simple—in Sweden, volunteers visit and help care for six aged people a day. Some jobs require great talent and training—the use of art as therapy for disturbed children. In addition to the development of imaginative new services to meet the critical community needs of which we are aware, we need to think of services which will serve to identify changing needs and to channel volunteers to immediately critical areas. What kinds of "clearing houses" now exist?

The volunteer should not be confused with the amateur. Well-planned volunteer work requires the full use of a woman's talents and abilities. It should draw upon her prior training and experience and offer new training, when needed, for the type of work that will be satisfying to her and useful to the community. We need more rigorous training programs for volunteers. What are the possibilities for cooperation between voluntary agencies and universities? Would it be possible to have programs of "career planning" for volunteers which would involve supervision and the keeping of personnel records that could be used later by other volunteer agencies, other communities, or by paying employers? Can a career planning program move volunteers into more responsible jobs as they acquire training and experience? Such volunteer work, which may indeed be interchangeable with paid work, should attract the most capable volunteer and at the same time provide part-time training and experience for the homemaker who needs to acquire or maintain her skills for the future.

In some professions volunteer activity is an integral part of the work experience. Doctors serve in clinics and lawyers in legal aid and voluntary defender organizations. Would not more rigorous training and career planning also elevate the status of the volunteer and thus attract more women of education, ability, and financial security to needed community service?

The need for guidance and training

We are beginning to examine the kinds of service and the kinds of education which will bring together the unused talent and the need for that talent. This conference is a reassuring example of the attention that is needed. It is going to be an enormous task. There will be no solution without skilled guidance for women—beginning early in life and continuing throughout. Our counseling programs must be brought in line with realities. Heretofore, school counselors often have been deterred in their counseling by the attitude of employers who restrict vocational opportunities for women and by negative public and personal attitudes toward their employment. Nevertheless, we find women serving in almost every trade, occupation, and profession. Counseling as well as training courses for girls should be planned realistically, taking into account the fact that most girls will work at some time in their lives, that most will also marry and have children, and that they need help, encouragement, and training to prepare them for combining these experiences in a practical time sequence.

Guidance is more than information about the increasing pattern of re-entry into the labor market after children are grown. We should not wait until the woman is thirty-five with three children in school before telling her what the future holds. The Women's Bureau study, *Fifteen Years After College: A Study of Alumnae of the Class of 1945,* has already uncovered widespread dissatisfaction with the extent and timing of guidance services. Early guidance and an understanding of the married woman's life pattern can point to areas which are flexible and to ways in which professional skills can be kept alive during the years at home. But very often a woman's interests may change. Margaret Rioch says in describing her program of training housewives to be mental health therapists: "Women who manage families and raise children have to be concerned with people, their development and their problems. Many women emerge from this training ground in interpersonal relations with considerable skill in deciphering unspoken messages, in handling tensions, and in helping people to develop their potentials."

Effective guidance can lead women into the kind of retraining and continuing education program represented by the Minnesota Plan, by The Center for Continuing Education of Sarah Lawrence, and the Radcliffe Institute for Independent Study. Guidance plays a part in all of these plans. In some, the heart of the plan is guidance toward effective use of the educational and training resources already plentifully available in the metropolitan area.

The keynote of all these centers is experimentation and variety. This is important since we are only at the threshold of the effort to reap the dividend on our investment in women's education. Some institutes stress job training. At Northeastern University, the director spent hundreds of hours canvassing businesses in the Boston vicinity to find out what their needs were and in the process helped educate them to the possibilities for flexible work schedules for well-trained women.

Continuing education is not only for the liberal arts major who has had a college education and wants to apply it. Many young girls graduate from high school, get married, and raise their families. What do we offer them when they have free time on their hands? The high school graduate can aspire to something more than a job in a laundry or on an assembly line. And in any event automation is going to eliminate many of these jobs.

The Federal Government has recognized some of these needs. The preamble to the Manpower Development and Training Act of 1962 states:

> The Congress finds that there is critical need for more and better trained personnel in many vital occupational categories, including professional, scientific, technical, and apprenticeable categories; that even in periods of high unemployment, many employment opportunities remain unfilled because of the shortage of qualified personnel; and that it is in the national interest that current and prospective manpower shortages be identified and that persons who can be qualified for these positions through education and training be sought out and trained, in order that the Nation may meet the staffing requirements of the struggle for freedom.

Women who undertake demanding education or new training for a job must be assured of equal opportunity and equal pay for work they do. Despite the increasing participation of women workers and the widening range of occupations in which they work, the majority of women are still in relatively few occupations; and the gap between the average earnings of men and women is widening. We are hopeful that the enactment and enforcement of Federal legislation, with its educational impetus, will remedy this situation.

For many women, higher education does not look toward a goal other than personal enrichment, and this is very important too. For many women, their first opportunity to go to college comes in the period of quiet when the children are grown. This is the time to survey the doors that can be opened. We need a great deal of experimentation in order to open the doors of higher education to mature women.

Traditionally women are geographically trapped. Married women must be able to commute to the place of study. The community college will have a growing importance both for mature women students and teachers. We can look with great interest upon experiments in extension courses. The Department of Agriculture has well developed techniques that can serve as guides for different types of programs. We welcome the experiment in a national testing service undertaken by the University of Chicago that will provide an objective standard for the success of home study and freer transfer of credits.

Conclusion

The needs of women and the needs of our society are not in opposition—quite the contrary. The need for the educated woman is acute; her need to contribute is strong. The opportunities are there; often they are subtle. Because of her special life pattern, because so often she is not the chief wage earner of the family, she can see the undefined job—the job that is not classified but that needs doing—and she can go out and do it. A society as rich as ours can afford to shape its demands in a way which takes account of her special needs. The Commission on the Status of Women, the Women's Bureau, the centers for continuing education, universities, the many articulate scholars and writers have all contributed to a climate of concern about the American woman. In all of this discussion we should keep in mind the goal that all people may enjoy richer more satisfying lives. This can be achieved if we develop and use the talent which is so abundant in our society.

REMARKS IN ELABORATION
OF WORKING PAPER

MRS. PETERSON: I am going to make just a few observations because we are short of time, and then I hope that we can begin the discussion. I think the needs of society and the needs of women are interwoven and intermixed. They are the needs of both. To see the needs of society, you have only to look around your community. I don't think you even have to read. You have to be sensitive, and you have to open your eyes and feel and see. There is no need for me to list these needs because you all know them. They are limitless—absolutely limitless. If there has ever been a time when we need the imagination, intelligence, and integrity of all of our people, it's now. I am not a psychiatrist; I am not a sociologist. But I do have the opportunity to see our needs and to participate in a society that is quite wonderful in the democratic way it tries to meet these needs. There is no easy answer. The problems are complex; the answers are many and complex. And I felt today we were dividing things up too much. They are not divided. The spectrum between man and woman *is* a spectrum, and the differential in sex is a spectrum. So the needs are there, and some people, such as Dr. Wilson in his welcoming speech, felt the needs of society were definite but that the needs of the woman were not as great. I think that the needs of the woman are much greater, and I have much personal experience to illustrate this, as well as letters that come to us and studies and inquiries that we make.

The need for skilled workers, for example, is very great. Whenever I visit a community, I spend some time, usually early in the morning, in the employment office. There I always find the unskilled group—large numbers of women who have to work and who have left school early. The proportion reads like a graph. In the part of the employment office where the unskilled jobs are being filled, the benches are full. I used to interview a sampling of these people, and in that sampling I found economic need first. I found lack of education second. And I found lack of training third. In the section where the semiskilled jobs are being filled, the benches are a little less crowded. In the skilled section, there is almost no one sitting on the benches. They don't even have to come in; they telephone. And of the professionals, the employers are there saying, "Please, send us the people." This is, I think, the situation in our society that we educators have to look at.

We had an amusing experience the other day when I was in

one of the employment offices. An employer called, stating his need for a mathematical computer. The interviewer, who took the call at the employment office, said, "Well, I have a person here that has just come in . . . a graduate with the following experience . . . ." The man said, "Oh, send him over immediately." The interviewer said, "It isn't a him, it's a her." And he said, "Oh, I don't know. Will this work?" She replied, "That is up to you." He was so desperate that he said, "Well, let me try." He did try, and when I called him back, he said, "She is superb. Please send me some more like her." Another employer called and said, "I need a man for something—or a good woman." So we have all these situations. It is important for us to recognize the reality of these grave needs, and we need the imagination of people and the willingness to experiment in new ways and in new directions to find new answers to these problems.

Last, I want you to know how strongly I feel about the importance of the small percent of women—the educated woman—that we're talking about. They provide the climate of opinion that makes possible the formation of ideas in our country. This cannot be underestimated. Their intelligent participation in the communities is one of the greatest needs that we have. To me it is a matter of social engineering. There are no built-in answers to the problem of automation or to our other problems. Their solution is going to take thinking and political awareness. How do we find, under our democratic system, the way to solve these problems? For example, let's take the temporary unemployment insurance bill. This bill—to help meet the problem of our economy today, to allow extended benefits to persons who have exhausted their benefits and cannot find work but who are looking for work—was defeated. The biggest argument against the bill that was used in the Ways and Means Committee was that a large number of persons who would qualify are women whom they term marginal employees or marginal workers and, therefore, not deserving and not needy. Now, here are two fallacies. In the first place, unemployment insurance is not based on need; it is based on one's attachment to the labor force. Second, the women who do qualify are not marginal workers. They are heads of families. They are women who are working to support themselves. They are not working for pin money. They are working for the same reasons that other people work all the time.

We must pinpoint these myths around us, I was called to the telephone this morning because I am working very hard on an equal pay bill in Congress which would say that a job is paid a certain amount regardless of who performs it. This would eliminate the situation where a man is paid more for performing a job than a woman performing the identical job. They telephoned me from the committee, asking if I would accept an amendment granting an additional allowance for the amount that it costs to employ a woman. Now, here I am faced with a policy decision based on a myth—on a myth about the value of women and how they work that is prevalent throughout our society. I thought immediately of the woman who came to me and said, "I have three children. I am a widow. I work in a bank. I get $15 a week less than a man right next to me who does identical work, although he has a wife working full time." You see, it is a myth that women cost more to employ.

Let's have research to investigate these myths thoroughly. We do not have all the facts. We find that there are individual differences with regard to matters such as absenteeism. All of these things depend on the person, but we have no evidence to show they are related to sex. I have studied myths associated with women who work in other countries and have found the same misconceptions. I'm thinking of one study that was done in Sweden on the effect on children of the employment of their mothers. It was found that the children of women who worked because of choice—who wanted to work—had the highest academic standing in the schools. The children who came from mothers who had to work because of economic necessity—who didn't want to work—had the lowest rate. So actually many possibilities exist, and I would appeal to you to tackle the problems on a realistic basis. Although educated women may constitute a small percent of the labor force, they play an essential role because they are the ones who will help determine the direction that our democracy will go.

DISCUSSION

Mr. McMahon: I would like to comment on a couple of myths that I think appear in your paper. I say this not to quibble with you but to keep the record straight because you seem to feel that certain opportunities are not available to women which some of us think are. For example, you say, "For many women, their first opportunity to go to college comes in the period of quiet when the children are grown." Obviously there is no home responsibility of a child-caring nature at that point so you say we need experimentation to open the doors of higher education for mature women. I would like to point out that 145 evening colleges belong to the Association of University Evening Colleges. So from coast to coast there are places where these mature women can go to get higher education.

Mrs. Peterson: That is true, but 145 is a very small number when you consider the large number of cities without evening colleges.

Mr. McMahon: Well, let us look at this factually because in the following paragraph you say that women are trapped geographically. Now we expect men to commute as many as forty to sixty miles to go to evening colleges. In my opinion, the man who works is just as trapped geographically as a woman. Let us grant that a woman should not drive in snow and ice for sixty miles. Maybe this is the difference for which there should be protection, but, nevertheless, my point is that there are many opportunities which exist that are overlooked in considering this problem. Second, I don't think a woman is more trapped geographically because of being married than is the man who is pinned to a job and a home.

Mrs. Peterson: I think she is more trapped geographically because of home responsibilities in her dual role.

Mrs. Antonia Chayes (Executive Secretary for the Committee on Education of the President's Commission on the Status of Women): I would like to answer further and say that when the children are grown and the husbands are at work all day, the daytime is a woman's free time. There may be 145 evening colleges, but I think there are not enough available even though the possibility of part-time college and graduate school education exists for some. I think the experiments at the University of Minnesota and at Sarah Lawrence show that the need is far greater than the supply. I don't think anyone could say that there are as many opportunities now as there could be.

CONFEREE: May I describe a woman I know—the woman of the future. She is an electronic physicist. She is employed by Sylvania, and when she had her first child, the personnel man suggested that she work part time. When the child was about a year old, she hired a good housekeeper and went back to work. Her pay was prorated, and she resumed her full-time research. She followed this pattern for three children.

MRS. PETERSON: This is possible and represents the kind of new thinking that we need. Another possibility is that of extending the working day beyond the normal nine to five. Some insurance companies have begun what they call a mother shift. Women who cannot work during the day because of small children work an evening shift that begins between six and seven and ends between ten and eleven. A number of manufacturers who are in need of certain types of skilled women are experimenting with this plan. Again I think we need to think constructively about new plans and face the fact that the old patterns have to give way.

MODERATOR: MISS MARY DONLON (Judge, United States Customs Court) : I am sorry to report that Mrs. Peterson must leave to catch a plane. Questions should be directed to the panel composed of Mrs. Antonia Chayes, executive secretary of the Committee on Education of the President's Commission on the Status of Women, and Miss Jean Wells, chief of the Branch of Labor Force Research, Women's Bureau.

MISS FLORENCE ANDERSON (Secretary of the Carnegie Corporation and of the Carnegie Foundation for the Advancement of Teaching) : I would like to ask what studies have been made on part-time work for women? Do you have any quantitative studies?

PANEL MEMBER: We put out a report recently that was based on census material and supplemented it with some studies of pertinent industry associations, manufacturers, and the like. We found that approximately one-third of the women in the labor force have part-time jobs, one-third have full-time jobs for the full year, and one-third work part of the year at full-time jobs. Therefore, only about one-third of the 24 million women in the labor force have jobs like men.

CONFEREE: Did you find any difference in the level of education between women holding part-time jobs and those holding full-time jobs?

PANEL MEMBER: My impression is that the education level of those working part-time is not very different from the education level of women in the labor force generally, where approximately 8 percent have a college degree. We found that the demand for women with professional training is great, and the supply is small. We receive a tremendous number of inquiries from women who say they wish that they could pursue their respective careers on a part-time basis. Working part time can be difficult, but these women could manage if they had more understanding from the employers. We in the Government say it is our policy to give women opportunities for part-time work, but when it comes to the actual fact, part-time work seems difficult to arrange. There is a book about part-time employment opportunities, however, that I think is still in manuscript form and will soon be published by Doubleday.

MRS. MARGARET HICKEY (Member, President's Commission on Status of Women and Chairman of its Committee on Federal Employment Policies and Practices) : It seems to me that we have a very real need to explore the problems of the educated woman with regard to society's need for her educational qualifications and the opportunities open to her. What are the demands for educated women? Are there projections that call for more educated women with graduate degrees to meet new needs?

PANEL MEMBER: As we go over the list of occupations we find nothing that women aren't going to be needed for. Just as there is a tremendous demand for teachers, so there are demands for nurses, for social workers, for all the health occupations, for librarians, for everything. The advice that we give to women who write in and ask questions like yours is that they should consider the entire gamut of available occupations and try to find out what is compatible with their temperament, abilities, and interests and then get the training necessary for that occupation. They are going to be needed in just about any field they choose, and the more education they have and the more they know about their field, the more they will be used and the happier they will be.

The College and the
Continuing Education of Women

Gordon W. Blackwell
President, Florida State University

THE SUBJECT OF "WOMAN" has eternally been a fascinating field of research for man, but unfortunately his scholarly efforts in this area have not been as distinguished as in others. Great have been his accomplishments in scholarly and scientific research, but the nature of woman leaves him confused and uncertain. He surveys the field, collects material, analyzes the data—and then usually reduces his subject to an object for deeper research. He pursues his study and finally decides with supreme assurance that he now knows all that can be known of "woman." And then he finds in his hands an enigma, a dynamic force which defies cataloguing and precise knowledge and leaves him wondering if this is not one natural phenomenon which will forever escape his control. Man's only consolation in such a dilemma is the realization that intuitive knowledge is often more rewarding and exhilarating than precise knowledge which has been proved and reduced to formula. If I might resort to poetic license, I would like to make a slight change in Sophocles' eulogy of man in his *Antigone:* "Wonders are many, and none is more wonderful than woman." Which brings me, in my own fashion, to the education of women.

Higher education for women is a comparatively new phenomenon in America. As we all know, the first woman was admitted to an institution of higher learning at Oberlin College in 1837, and in the intervening 125 years women have made remarkable and miraculous use of the opportunities for which they fought so valiantly. It was natural that the pioneers in this movement—the first women to attend college and the many fine women's colleges which came into existence in the East and South—would establish for women the right to pursue the same curricula as pursued by men to prove that women had the toughness of mind and the intellectual capacity to master any academic discipline. This battle has long since been won by women; the frontier of education for women has been conquered. We have reached a point where Ashley Montagu, a noted social anthropologist, has had the audacity and the courage to publish a treatise entitled *The Natural Superiority of Women,* which has been reluctantly accepted as truth by men as well as women! We are, therefore, now able to move from the proving ground to the experimental in the field of education for women and to examine without emotionalism the possibility that women may have peculiar needs which could demand, in part at least, a different kind—though not a different quality—of education from that required for men.

As we discuss the continuing education of women, let us note a position stated by John Gardner: "Our educational purposes must be seen in the broader framework of our convictions concerning the worth of the individual and the importance of individual fulfillment . . . what we must reach for is a conception of perpetual self-discovery, perpetual reshaping to realize one's goals, to realize one's best self, to be the person one could be."[1] When we give special attention to the continuing education of women, I suppose in the words of Gardner we are assuming that the process of "perpetual self-discovery, perpetual reshaping to realize one's goals, to realize one's best self, to be the person one could be" is different in some ways for women than for men in American society. Furthermore, certain of these sex differences account for the several types of adult women for whom we should provide continuing educational opportunities. Since the average age of marriage for women is now twenty and since the woman more frequently than the man drops out of education when marriage occurs, there are many women of intellectual ability whose college education was interrupted by marriage or who did not go to college at all. After leaving college some women begin a career only to interrupt it for marriage and child rearing. Many are now ready to return to gainful employment. Others have gone into marriage and child rearing immediately

[1] John W. Gardner, "The Servant of All Our Purposes" (New York: Carnegie Corporation of New York, 1959), pp. 1–2.

after high school but now desire to enter a career for the first time. Still others have had no work experience and do not desire a career because of personal inclination or a secure economic situation; for these, opportunities for liberal studies constitute their continuing educational need.

So much, then, for an introduction to the problem. My paper has two main parts. First I feel it necessary to say something about the education of college women because of the potential significance of these experiences for continuing education after the college years. Then I shall address myself to possibilities and problems facing the college in the continuing education of adult women.

Experiences in the college years

The counseling they receive in college directly affects the education of women after they leave the campus. (I might add that counseling in high school is also extremely important in this respect.) Adequate counseling should help the young woman come to understand the nature of life patterns and roles which lie ahead of her, the social stereotypes relative to women which are part of American culture and society, and the career opportunities which will be open to her. The young woman needs help in considering the next twenty to forty years so that she can more clearly perceive what the future may hold. For example, she should hear discussion of alternate patterns of study, marriage, and careers. She should see the possible variations for a girl of her age and with her particular intellectual capacities and career interests who wants a home and children. There are many alternatives. She could complete her college degree, work for a few years, marry and have children, then later return to study through refresher programs in a college (perhaps by television or programmed home learning), and eventually engage in her chosen profession for another twenty to twenty-five years. Or she could leave college after two years, marry and rear children, then return to complete a college education (again possible through TV, home study, and some resident work), and finally enter upon her career. And, of course, there could be several variations of these patterns.

Discussing these sorts of life patterns with professional counselors, the woman college student can be prepared more intelligently and more realistically to make decisions at certain choice points which lie ahead for her. Such counseling should impress upon the student the importance of developing her intellectual and creative talents to the utmost, first for the benefit of an increasingly complex society and its demand for responsible citizens and competent workers, both technical and professional, and second for her own personal fulfillment. Directing attention of the student to women members of the faculty as role models can be helpful in this connection. Also the intellectually superior women students (as well as the men) should be encouraged in the freshman year to begin to give serious thought to future graduate study and college teaching as a career.

Furthermore, the student should come to understand and develop a commitment to the idea that education must be a continuing process, something like a bus trip on which one may get off at any stop or continue to the end of the line. The rewards and satisfactions, both personal and monetary, in continuing one's education should be made clear.

But if we stop with providing specialized counseling for college women, we shall have missed several other opportunities. What we must do for the undergraduate woman student is to augment her educational opportunities on the campus and begin to build an intellectual bridge between the undergraduate years and later opportunity for continuing education. A first step should be to remove any barriers which may exist to the most effective possible undergraduate education of women. For example, scholarly achievement by women should be given a place of prestige in the culture of the student body. Special awards and recognitions may be offered for women students as one means of achieving this goal.

Our young people are among the most mobile group in the most mobile population of the world. The wife who married young and whose husband's work requires frequent moves often finds it necessary to study at several colleges before completing a degree. Discussions with student wives reveal the need for greater flexibility in the acceptance of transfer credits toward requirements of a college degree. In this connection some method of testing achievement in college work, particularly at the end of the sophomore year, is urgently needed, and it is encouraging that the Educational Testing Service is well along in the development of such an instrument. The time may come when we will have sufficient confidence in standardized testing to assign as much weight to these test scores as to the accumulation of formal course credits which often are difficult to evaluate. Such test data, incidentally, would help in decisions concerning the admission of women transfer students.

There are, of course, certain educational programs which are especially suited to women because certain occupations are differentially open to them. Furthermore, some educators maintain that a special kind of orientation course for women is needed in college, perhaps one focusing upon the life patterns of women in American society. Such a course with academically respectable content can be developed as more and more research is becoming available on these matters. There is a danger, however, that a course designed especially for women may be superficial. In fact, I know of such a required course which is little more than a how-to-do-it discussion of feminine charm, yet academic credit is given.

Finally, I would emphasize the importance of the alumni office in its contacts with students during their senior year. This is the time for the college to make a proper beginning in a continuing relationship with alumni and alumnae on an intellectual basis. Some colleges have found it effective to have a faculty-administration committee to focus attention on the education of women and to stimulate further efforts to provide maximum opportunities for women within the institution.

Educational counseling centers for women

Having discussed the responsibilities of the college (and I include the university as well) for making their undergraduate women students ready for continuing education, we turn now to a consideration of problems and possibilities in providing continuing educational opportunities for them. Here there is a clear need for educational counseling centers for women. There are few places where women of thirty or forty or even fifty years of age can go for diagnosis of their intellectual potential, evaluation of their prior education, and review of their work experience, with subsequent counseling as to next steps in both education and career. Many of these women were in high school or college before Pearl Harbor, before atomic energy was harnessed, before man ventured into space. They find themselves in a different social environment in which opportunities for women have greatly expanded. With children in school or college and with the freedom from household chores provided by modern technology, they frequently feel a growing restlessness and antipathy toward mental and physical inactivity. They see about them evidences of an increasing acceptability of women in a wide variety of working roles. Their husbands, as well as their employers and other men in society, show signs of accepting this new role of women, and, in fact, frequently are anxious to accept them in partnership in other than home and family concerns. Furthermore, the chances are that they will outlive their husbands.

In the face of these aspects of modern society, women with more and more time on their hands are often anxious to seek new modes of personal development and social contribution. Inquiries made daily at colleges and universities, the popularity of adult education courses, the continuing invasion of the job market—all these attest the need of women to find ways of becoming and remaining genuinely active and productive. Whether for personal satisfaction, for enhancing employability and productive potential, or for learning to fill better a voluntary community leadership role, many women have revealed that they see a first step toward self-fulfillment in a return to education.

Adult women will bring these kinds of questions to an educational counseling center: What is my intellectual aptitude or potential? What professional or technical work should I prepare for? Based on the education I have had, what kind of educational program do I now need? What kind of general or liberal courses should I take to be intellectually and culturally alive? From what institution can I get the required educational program and through what medium—resident study for one or more years, occasional resident courses, resident summer session, correspondence courses, television courses, or programmed learning in the home?

These inquiries about continuing education, however, also reveal a number of problems. The need for some intellectual exercise manifests itself, it would seem, as a vague but persistent uneasiness; pathways for easement are not so well traveled that the woman can easily examine a number of routes, determine where they might lead, and carry through on a choice to follow one or another. In other words, the trails are not so well blazed that they may be followed by many without a guide.

It is also apparent that further formal college course work, though sometimes available in evening colleges, is too often tailored to the needs and patterns of younger persons. The college, busy finding places and faculty for its expanding enrollment, generally has been a poor resource for aiding the older woman. Should the college give wide publicity to the courses likely to appeal to her, she would still be reluctant to return to the classroom. Her hesitancy points to the need for facilities to evaluate academic ability, for good descriptions of available educational opportunities, and for information concerning the levels of competitiveness in academic courses.

Because the man has been the usual breadwinner, educational guidance research and practices have been developed from a largely masculine point of view. Although one may find guidance agencies for other special groups, such as the aged, the handicapped, or racial groups, counseling or guidance agencies set up exclusively for women are rare. Because of heavy male case loads, the existing agencies have had little time to devote to the specialized educational guidance problems of women, despite the unique needs to be served. There are challenging guidance problems arising out of the particular roles of women in culture, attitudinal barriers to their employment in certain fields, and the general question of the productive utilization of education by women.

Guidance research should undertake the development of diagnostic devices specifically designed for adult women. With such instruments available, considerable research will be required to provide valid norms and other reliable bases for effective counseling. Furthermore, a concerted effort should be made to recruit and train middle-aged women counselors, since such individuals may be able to relate more directly to the needs and problems of these clients.

Since educational choices are frequently determined by vocational problems, the educational counseling center should also be equipped to provide help to the counselees in relating possible educational programs to their vocational needs. The center would not serve as a job placement agency, however, except as problems in these areas relate to educational decisions. Neither would its function include personal counseling or therapy.

A secondary but important function of such a center would be to discover and develop opportunities for continuing education within existing institutions which might be profitably opened to women and to ascertain the value and suitability of such programs for adult women. Follow-up studies of persons placed in various educational programs would be conducted as a guide for the counselor and counselee. Such educational counseling centers for women would help salvage considerable intellectual potential among women and channel it into helpful lines of development.

Problems and possibilities
in the continuing education of women

We turn now to consideration of what the college can do directly to meet the educational needs of adult women. One immediately encounters a number of roadblocks.

First, there is the matter of policy relative to admission of adult women students. Some college trustees and administrators seem to have a built-in adolescent bias and a corollary prejudice against mixing adults with regular students of so-called college age. In some instances there are unfavorable faculty attitudes toward adult women as students. When the woman who has not attended college for a number of years applies for admission, there are difficulties in determining the current adequacy of her previous work, whether for credit toward an undergraduate degree or for fulfilling the prerequisites for graduate study.

Then there is the problem of scheduling classes for the convenience of women with household responsibilities. As institutions begin to schedule classes throughout the day and into the evenings, this difficulty is minimized. Furthermore, academic attitudes toward degree credit for correspondence study, television courses, and programmed learning in home study must be kept flexible, and experimentation along these lines should be encouraged.

As to curriculum, again we say that most of the continuing educational programs and course work should probably be the same for women as for men. For example, several institutions now offer bachelor's or master's programs in general studies to meet adult interests in liberal education rather than in specific career preparation. But there are certain programs, such as nursing and home economics, which have special appeal for women. Furthermore, good results have been obtained in several programs designed to prepare adult women for teaching mathematics.

Many universities have a firm commitment to extend instructional services beyond the campus. Aside from the national home demonstration extension program, not much has been done that is pointed directly toward the educational needs of women. General extension is one of the largest areas of opportunity still to be developed in the continuing education of women. Imagination is needed for the development of new kinds of university organization which will no longer make extension a function viewed as somewhat apart from the other functions of the university. We need new kinds of administrative machinery to integrate the continuing education function with regular on-campus teaching and research. Rather than weakening or diluting these basic functions of a university, I believe that relating the research and teaching faculty to problems and activities in continuing education can have beneficial results.

I have already noted that the alumni office, working closely with academic departments, has an opportunity and a responsibility to develop and maintain continuing contacts of an intellectual sort with the alumni and alumnae. While the first response may come from former students with marked intellectual ability, I would hope that increasingly all alumni would be involved.

Articles of intellectual import should be carried by the alumni magazine, and alumni offices can provide annual reading lists. Though most suggested readings would be the same for men as for women, some lists specifically for women would be helpful. Faculty lectures at homecoming and other alumni meetings are becoming common.

Again, the idea of alumni or alumnae seminars for a long week end or even for a week or two is catching hold. At the Woman's College of the University of North Carolina we invited fifty graduates of the past ten years who had made good academic records to return to the campus for a two-and-a-half day alumnae seminar on modern philosophies. The response was enthusiastic with more than thirty attending, some from as far away as eight hundred miles. A number brought their husbands who participated fully. The reaction was universally favorable; some of the women emphasized that this was the kind of relationship which the college should establish with its alumnae. Incidentally, contributions to the alumnae fund from this particular group increased many-fold! Alumnae programs such as this are particularly important because they provide for women some of the opportunities in liberal adult education that business and industry are making available to management personnel but which in effect are primarily for men. Moreover, the alumnae seminars may focus on topics of special concern for women. The pioneering work of Vassar College in this kind of continuing education has demonstrated these points.

Assistance from outside the college or university

I would like further to suggest that there are ways through which colleges can be aided in expanding the continuing educational opportunities for women. I have two examples, one at the state-wide level and one for coordination and stimulation nationally.

In a number of states, efforts to coordinate higher education on a state-wide basis present new and unique opportunities in continuing education.[2] For example, in Michigan and Ohio, public

[2] See T. R. McConnell, *A General Pattern for American Public Higher Education* (New York: McGraw-Hill Book Co., 1962), chap. viii.

and private institutions of higher education through voluntary cooperation have developed a master plan for higher education in the state. In still other states, such as California, Florida, New Mexico, New York, and Texas, there is official coordinating machinery for the state-supported institutions. A master plan for state-supported higher education has already been blueprinted in California and New York. Florida is currently engaged in a role and scope study which will result in an allocation of functions to the several state universities. In each of these state-wide efforts continuing education is given consideration, but it is doubtful that particular attention has been devoted to the educational needs of adult women.

Particular note should be made of the recent establishment of the Florida Institute for Continuing University Studies. This new agency has a director with the status of a university president. The institute serves as the system-wide agency through which the state universities extend their programs and services to off-campus locations. Voluntary cooperation with private colleges is anticipated. If the institute and one or more of the state universities in Florida should decide that special attention must be given to the educational needs of adult women, administrative machinery is available to attack this program imaginatively on a state-wide basis. It may be noted that California and Oregon also have a state-wide structure for coordination of general extension, though with what appears to be less centralization of authority and administration than is the pattern in Florida.

At the national level, the American Council on Education, through its Commission on the Education of Women, showed what can be accomplished with minimum financing in the coordination and stimulation of efforts to extend and improve the education of women, including continuing education. The commission provided a national focus of interest on this segment of higher education. Through an effective newsletter, which is now published by the American Association of University Women, a clearinghouse function was established. My own experience in two institutions has indicated that there is considerable administrative and faculty interest in this newsletter. The commission planned and conducted several conferences pertaining to selected aspects of the education of women such as the one we are now having. Furthermore, staff and members of the commission were able to stimulate interest in research concerning the education of women.

It is my opinion that the commission performed a helpful service to colleges and educational organizations, as well as to philanthropic foundations, news media, and women's organizations seeking a worthy cause. I firmly believe its reactivation is warranted by the nationwide interest which has been shown in the education of women, by the urgency of the special educational needs involved, and by the constructive experience of the commission during the several years of its existence. It is my hope that necessary funds will be provided for the re-establishment of this commission.

Conclusion

I would like finally to go beyond the purview of my assigned topic and suggest that the time has now come for action in the education of women. Through the studies of the Commission on the Education of Women and the Women's Bureau of the Department of Labor, through conferences such as this one in which we are participating, and through the research of individual social scientists and other scholars, we have dissected woman and her needs—personally, educationally, and professionally. We have come to the conclusion that the peculiar life cycles of women, the multiple roles which they must play in modern society, and their needs for self-fulfillment—intellectually and professionally—require special kinds of education. Some of these needs may be met by the institution of higher learning in its general educational program but other needs must be met with special programs for women. Some enterprising institutions have established specific opportunities for women such as the Program for Continuing Education of Women at the University of Minnesota and the Radcliffe plan for independent and creative research for able women. But not enough has been done, and the efforts of most of us are sporadic.

The American Association of University Women, perhaps the greatest influence in our country for quality education for women, has a slogan which seems to me apropos: "Action without study is folly, but study without action is futile." We have studied, we have analyzed, and we have concluded. The time is now here for action. Lest I hear the whisper, "Physician, heal thyself," I hasten to state that last spring I appointed at my own university a Committee on the Education of Women. This committee is at work to find ways of improving our contribution to the education of our women students and our alumnae. This may not be the answer for other institutions and organizations, but it is a method of implementation which gives me the courage to suggest that each should take whatever step is appropriate to his own situation, a step which will translate study into action.

REMARKS IN ELABORATION
OF WORKING PAPER

Mr. Blackwell: I think it is to be expected that many of the things that I had in my paper and that I might say now have already been touched upon in this conference. I think we could not discuss the topics that were on the agenda without getting over into things which the colleges and universities are doing or should be doing. I will just remind you of a few of the points I made in the paper.

I talked first about the importance of the college years for the continuing education of the young women who do have some opportunity in college, whether or not they graduate. Counseling and guidance assumes real importance in this regard. A number of down-to-earth facts can be helpful if communicated to women in the counseling process. They have been touched upon—the alternative patterns that might be ahead for the women or, as someone else called them, expectations. The sequence in which she can engage in these life patterns vary. My experience in talking to college women has been that they have not allowed for these possibilities, but when confronted with statistics about the number of years the average college woman will work, they see things a little differently. So I believe that counseling and guidance at this level is important. I am disturbed that fewer women seem to be going into guidance, and those who do, I feel, are prepared primarily to give guidance to the male students. I merely point out this wide area where the colleges are falling down and could do much better. Again, research is needed on this.

It seems to me there are certain barriers to the undergraduate education of women in our colleges that we might try to remove. I refer to the student culture in which intellectual achievement on the part of the woman is played down. This may be less true in the women's colleges but quite true I fear in many of the co-educational institutions, and we should do something about modifying this part of the student culture. I suggest that we need to be much more flexible in accepting transfer credits toward a degree. And we should do this for men as well, although women students seem to be more mobile for they follow their husbands who often move from job to job. This presents real difficulties in completing a college degree. I agree with President Wilson when he said that in this respect we are most conservative at the college or university. We need much more flexibility. I take the position that it is not the difference in content so much that we need in the education of women, although an occasional special course for women might be necessary. I would shy away from an orientation course at the freshman level, but a seminar later in the college experience of a woman, dealing with the results of research about the roles of women in American life, might be very helpful.

No one has mentioned the alumni office and its role. I would like to emphasize that as the alumni office gets away from promoting football only and begins to develop continuing intellectual contacts with the alumni, much can be done. And I feel that the alumni office should focus particularly on the problem of the education of women and her opportunities. One way a college or university can approach this matter of removing some of the barriers to the education of women is a faculty administration committee appointed to study the matter and to see that there is follow-up action taken in the institution.

As to the responsibility of the institution in the continuing education of women after they have left the campus, I suggest the importance of education counseling centers for adult women. My experience has been that when a woman goes back to the regular college or university counseling center, she usually is greeted with a stony stare, or if the counselors want to be helpful, they don't know how. So it seems to me that we should at least experiment in a few places with an education counseling center focusing upon the needs of adult women. I would like to see some demonstration projects on this type of counseling center conducted by foundations with built-in research and evaluative devices, so we can determine whether this idea is worthwhile. Most women who have had only a year or two of college work or none at all are hesitant and somewhat frightened about the prospect of going back to college. They do not know how to evaluate their ability now or how to evaluate the schooling they have had in the past. And too often the college is not able to evaluate their past schooling either. This is one function that an educational counseling center might perform. I warn against such a center's becoming a job placement agency and against its becoming a place for women to bring their personal problems. You have to screen out the personal problem cases that will certainly come to such a center and focus on educational counseling.

As a college or university tries to meet the needs of adult women, certain roadblocks will be encountered. Too often, I fear, admissions policies are such that the adult woman is not admitted or her admission is made difficult, or prejudice is expressed against part-time students. The faculty often objects to adult women in class. Someone asked this morning if you could mix adult women with undergraduate students. Certainly you can in some courses. Child development was suggested. I did it in a course in community organization and leadership and found that several mature women with a group of undergraduate women was a perfect combination. The mature women gave case studies of the things I was trying to talk about. It worked fine in that kind of course, and I believe it would work quite satisfactorily in most courses. Someone mentioned this morning that class scheduling might be inconvenient for women. I think that we have to schedule classes throughout the day and evening to give women the opportunity to take courses at either time of day.

One glaring omission in my paper, which I will mention before Ernest McMahon does, is the role of the evening colleges. The evening colleges—and the junior colleges—can perform important roles. A good place for a mature woman to be reintroduced to the academic process is near her home, and junior colleges are now being created near most homes in this country. University extension programs are important, too, and I pay my respects to the very real possibilities of correspondence work, of television work, and of programmed home study. I don't know how long it will be before the colleges and universities will give credit for this work on the basis of efficiency examinations. This calls for more flexibility in our academic institutions.

I conclude by saying that I feel the Commission on the Education of Women of the American Council on Education has performed a very real service and that a similar group is needed to sponsor future meetings such as this, to provide some coordination of the many different kinds of people in this very complex field, and to perform a clearinghouse function. Finally, I suggest that in our own institutions and organizations we should really gear for action.

DISCUSSION

Mrs. Eunice Roberts (Assistant Dean for Undergraduate Development for Women's Educational Programs, Indiana University) : I want to take issue with our speaker on one point. I do not believe it is true that a woman student does not want to appear to be a good student. In my judgment, the woman student in the coeducational institution is just as proud of high scholarship as the man student, and there is a good deal of evidence to substantiate this.

Mr. Blackwell: This may well be. I think it is an area in which we need further research. I am sure there are some instances that would bear out my generalization, but that is not enough, of course.

Mr. Seymour Smith (President, Stephens College) : I would like to raise a question about a matter that has been bothering me throughout the discussions so far. I feel we have been dealing with these questions in a rather segmented fashion—here a little piece and there a little piece. We have been talking about the continuing education of women. You have been talking about it on the undergraduate level in terms of giving perspective to a younger woman. I don't think this can be done by guidance and counseling only, nor could it be done by force, but it is going to be done by the means that Dr. Rothwell mentioned. The campus culture, counseling, the attitudes of the faculty members, courses, the extracurricular enterprises, the residence hall program—all must help the girl realize that she has a long life ahead and that she must plan for it. If we are going to do a good job in an undergraduate college we had better be thinking in these comprehensive terms.

You have discussed adult education and continuing education for adult women. We have identified a variety of needs which are quite different. On the one hand, the goal of continuing education is to stimulate intellectual capacity; on the other hand, its goal is to update persons for vocations and a variety of other things. These different objectives are not going to be done through any single approach but through a variety of approaches, and I want to ask if we are going to formulate a long-range strategy in which an institution plans both on the undergraduate and postgraduate level. Such long-range planning would include motivation of women as well.

Mr. BLACKWELL: I quite agree, and I would say that if an institution does some soul searching when making its plans, the results will depend a great deal on the type of institution and its own personality as an institution. I mentioned junior colleges. I think there is something they can do that is very different from a four-year girls' college. The situation is very different, again, at a large university with a national reputation. The answers will have to be worked out individually for each institution. The sites of institutions vary. The urban institution has different opportunities from the university located in a rural area.

Mrs. SENDERS: I wanted to add one point to what you have said this afternoon. Even if an institution has many or all of the things that you hope it would have—counseling facilities, efficient examinations, reasonable attitudes toward the transfer of credit, an active college—one other thing desperately needed is publicity.

The services and facilities can be there, but if the community does not know of them, they are not going to serve the function that they should.

MR. CARROLL: I wonder if the American Council on Education could look into the problem of the transfer of credit and that whole bundle of related problems which are greater, I believe, for women than for men, for the simple reason that men tend to complete their educational process because they have a vocational objective that has to be met, whereas many women have interruptions in their education and frequently do not return to the same institution in which they started.

MR. BLACKWELL: I should say at least one thing in defense of the academic point of view—especially the view concerning graduate credit. I think the universities and the colleges have an obligation to determine what credit means and that it should mean the same throughout the academic world. There can be different requirements to get credit, but the concept of credit has some value. In fact the standards of American higher education have been built up because of this concept of valid credits. The use of proficiency examinations is something that has become acceptable, at least on the professional level, but I wouldn't want to take the position that we should throw out the traditional concept of credit nor encourage you to think that it could be done. The movement toward proficiency examinations in New York was mentioned, and I think this can gain acceptance. But once we talk about academic credit at the graduate level, I suppose I would become a little bit conservative.

MISS GRACE HENDERSON (Dean, College of Home Economics, Pennsylvania State University): I would like to make a point related to counseling and to the statement that the university or college must let people know of the facilities available. Universities are not only interested in continuing education for credit, they are also interested in an informal type of continuing education. I mention this because, as an adult educator, I have come to believe that if education could do only one thing it should be to help people recognize their potentials and realize them far beyond what they are now doing. Just before coming here, I received a letter from a woman who said, "I hope your conference is going to pay some attention to this matter. There are women who know what they want. They recognize they want education, they go out and get it, and then they get a job. This is fine, but I believe there are large numbers of us who just have a sense of uneasiness. We're not quite sure what we want. We're not even sure that the uneasiness may not come from looking at our friends who are doing other things and thinking perhaps we ought to be doing something too. I wish discussion groups could be organized in communities all over this country as a result of your conference, which would bring women together to identify their own motives and to identify, if possible, their own potential abilities, and from this point, then, they could move." It also seems to me that this is a part of a responsibility of most alert institutions, that they help their citizens recognize their educational needs.

MR. DONALD MCNEIL (Collaborator on the study "The Role of the University in Adult Education") : I am doing a study with Dr. Fred Harrington of the University of Wisconsin on the role of the university in adult education. In the light of these last remarks, I thought it might be worthwhile to comment on the situation we found when we visited presidents, members of governing boards, members of state legislatures, foundation groups —all of the people directly or indirectly connected with adult education or continuing education. Our findings apply as much to continuing education for women as they do to the education of the rest of the population. Generally the situation is this. It was our impression that the top administration in most American universities and colleges gave lip service to continuing education. They talked a good deal about continuing education, but when we examined budgets and allocation of resources and when we talked to faculty members and heard their reaction to extension people or evening college people and saw the contempt with which adult educators or continuing education people are viewed by traditional faculty members, we came to the conclusion that someone is playing a hoax on someone else and that the people who are suffering are the clients. The problem originates with presidents and vice-presidents and deans who talk a good game, but when the time comes to put out money and time to build a program, to sell the idea of life-long learning which does not stop at age twenty-five or with a degree, most of them do nothing. When you do find a university president who takes an interest and believes in the idea, you have the exception that proves the rule elsewhere in the country.

Pilot Projects for
Continuing Education for Women

Margaret Habein Merry, *moderator*
Director of Admissions, Radcliffe College

MRS. MERRY: Tonight I am going to give the members of the panel a chance to say a few words about their programs. But before we get to the directors, I'm going to call on "our case history," Mrs. Lyda Boyer, who has been through continuing education at the University of Minnesota. She was a student of the Minnesota Plan, a graduate of "seminars," and is now enrolled in the degree program.

A CASE HISTORY

MRS. LYDA BOYER: I was asked to give a thumbnail sketch which would include my educational background, the intervening years, my connection with the Minnesota Plan, my re-entry into the University of Minnesota this fall, and, if possible, my goals for the future.

My college education began in 1937 at Brigham Young University. I enrolled as a physical education major simply because my high school instructor in physical education thought I had great talent as a dancer and had arranged for me to teach tap dancing to defray part of my tuition expenses. For two years I met the basic requirements as an undergraduate and, in addition, took every dancing class they had to offer. Some time during my junior year I decided that I really was not interested in physical education as a major and switched to a sociology major with an emphasis on social casework. At the end of my junior year I was married and went to the University of Wisconsin with my husband, who had a scholarship to work on his Ph.D. Our plan was that I would work for three years using my bread-and-butter skills—shorthand, typewriting, and bookkeeping—and by saving our pennies, I would go to the university during our fourth year and receive my bachelor's degree when my husband received his Ph.D. This plan might have worked out except that when I went to enroll at the University of Wisconsin during the beginning of our fourth year, I was dismayed to find that in making the transfer I lost so many credits that it would be absolutely impossible to finish my degree in one year's work. One of the main reasons for losing credits, of course, was my switch in major. However, I decided to enroll full time in upper-division work in sociology. I was one of four students chosen for a practical program with the Family Welfare Society in Madison, training students for social casework. I was assigned three cases and energetically entered into my new program.

I did not enroll the second semester in Wisconsin because the first of our three children was on her way. I was not feeling very well and I also I was disappointed that I would not be able to accomplish my goal and receive the degree. As an alternative, I contacted Brigham Young University and told them of my many problems with the transfer of credits, and we worked out an arrangement whereby I would take correspondence work from Brigham Young University under their direction, return for one summer session, and complete my bachelor's degree there.

At the end of that year my husband accepted his first academic position at Stanford, and our first child was born. The intervening years included Stanford University, World War II, three children, moving to Minnesota, and many other things as well. I am not eager to pass over these intervening years as unimportant, for they relate to my education as a woman, and that is in no way unimportant. The many activities that I have engaged in during this fifteen- or twenty-year span have had a significant impact upon my over-all education, my attitudes, and my interests today.

Thirteen years ago we moved just outside St. Paul to a new suburban neighborhood with a population of about 6,000 and one schoolhouse with four rooms. Since we moved there, the population has grown to over 25,000. I immediately plunged into suburban living and the problems entailed in the rapid growth of our village.

One of the first problems was the school situation. I became involved in a fund-raising bond issue for the purchase of land and the construction of school buildings. I became immersed in local, regional, and national PTA activities; most of them centering around finance and curriculum. And here I want to justify this area of endeavor for a woman's work. The parent groups in our PTA have had a significant effect in many concrete ways. For instance, two years ago we were effective in getting a raise across the board for teacher's salaries in our school district over the recommendations of the school board. We have had significant success in curriculum, in foreign language classes, and in mathematics classes. I have been a school election judge for many years and have worked closely with the superintendent in special assignments. I have given an endless number of lectures at our high school on local government, the state constitution, the United Nations, and on a recent trip my husband and I made to Russia.

Another area of activity that I should mention is the League of Women Voters. Besides helping to organize the first League of Women Voters in Roseville, I served as one of its early presidents. During this time we promoted village planning for our village and hired a professional planner to carry through with the plans. We had a marked effect on such things as building zones, zoning regulations, and building requirements. I have served on the recreation board for several years, helped organize the first girl scout troop in Roseville, and served as a girl scout leader and a cub scout den mother.

This brings me to my connection with the Minnesota Plan. You can see that I believe in the volunteer efforts of women. I do not belittle them in any way, but I must say that I was reaching the point where it was a little uncomfortable for me to call my friends and hear the pause at the end of the line while they waited for me to ask them for money or for service. Also I began to have uneasy feelings when my telephone rang, and I was asked to perform an endless number of services because I was a "good, willing worker." In addition, I had more and more free time. Our older girl was a sophomore in college, another a senior in high school, and our boy was in ninth grade. I could see the years stretching ahead of me, and I knew they would be quite different from my mother's years. I think that by the time their last child was in college and of marriageable age women of my mother's age no longer had the health and vitality for continued activity that we have today. Quite frankly, I was not happy with the thought of continuing with my voluntary activities and was casting around for some outlet, when Mrs. Cless, co-director of the Minnesota Plan, invited me to be a pilot member of its first seminar. This was in 1959, and we called our seminar "Critical Thinking in Contemporary Issues." It is now the New World of Knowledge Seminar. This seminar was exciting and stimulating for every woman who participated, and we were the envy of the professional men on campus who recognized the value and tremendous stature of the men giving these seminars.

I followed the first seminar with a second one, Arts of Reading, and a third one last year, Frontiers in Twentieth-Century Science. I have met the requirements for credit in these three seminars and made full use of Vera Schletzer, a counselor in the Minnesota Plan, in organizing and planning my courses.

Last fall I enrolled in the College of Science, Literature, and the Arts at the University of Minnesota and encountered some difficulty in getting my credits evaluated. I have had a scattered education, with credits from three universities as a student in residence, credits for correspondence work and as an adult special, and credits for the seminars in the extension division. At this point, I have no clear-cut goals or a definite major. I am sure my record must look horrid to an administrator who likes to see clear-cut goals and requirements filled. But I felt that I was welcome at the University of Minnesota and that the university officials were sympathetic and glad to have me there.

Some of the courses that I had taken at Brigham Young University and the University of Wisconsin were no longer listed in the catalogues so the officials didn't know whether to assign upper-division or lower-division credits to them. In many cases lower-division credits were assigned to the upper-division work that I so badly needed. Brigham Young University was not listed as an accredited school for correspondence work, and I needed their upper-division classes. I had to act as a guinea pig in getting my credits from the Minnesota Plan accepted in the College of Science, Literature, and the Arts. But with the help of understanding people, all of this has been accomplished. I am enrolled this fall, and I expect to have my bachelor's degree by June. I am sorry that I have no clear-cut goals at this time, but to have completed this degree will be a source of great satisfaction. Maybe with a little guidance and understanding I can acquire some definite goals and make concrete plans for the future.

MRS. MERRY: I think you will agree with me that this is quite a case history. Thank you very much, Mrs. Boyer.

I would like to ask Jane Berry, director of the University of Kansas City Project for Continuing Education of Women, to make some observations on the program there.

[Miss Berry's comments follow her working paper.]

UNIVERSITY OF KANSAS CITY

Project for
Continuing Education of Women

Jane Berry, *director*

THE UNIVERSITY OF KANSAS CITY Project for Continuing Education of Women was initiated in the fall of 1961 to:

1. Discover the needs for continuing education of women in the Kansas City area.
2. Plan, on the basis of well-considered research findings, experimental continuing education courses to fill identified educational needs of women in the Kansas City area.
3. Present special programs and symposia on current problems concerning the education of women.
4. Provide the basis for further study and research aimed at

long-range planning and guidance of special educational programs for women.

The philosophy of the University of Kansas City project is at present best characterized as one of experimentation. Research and program plans to date are regarded as pilot efforts designed to provide guidance and direction for further experimentation. These efforts will lead to the development of a substantial and sustaining program that will enable the university to serve the educational needs of women in a more comprehensive manner than is now possible.

From the inception of the project, we have been concerned about creating a climate both in the community and at the university which will encourage and facilitate the educational aspirations of women who have done some college work.

A unique feature of this project is the research forums[1] on women's education. These are day programs designed to bring together women of the community to consider continuing education of women and related problems. The format for the forums has consisted of general presentations by educators and behavioral scientists, followed by small group discussions in which the women have had an opportunity to discuss topics such as:

1. What can women do with an education?
2. Can women be both persons and mothers?
3. How do women perceive their life roles and opportunities?
4. Can women change the patterns of their lives?

The group discussions were recorded, and transcriptions have been analyzed. The following statements summarize the consensus of concerns of the women who participated:

1. The majority of women expressed a feeling that their formal education had been helpful, but they were *not* able to be specific about how particular courses of study contributed to what they are doing now.
2. Many of the women view education for personal development as the acquisition of specific skills with immediate utility

---

[1] Two of these forums have been held to date, and a third is tentatively planned for 1963. The first forum was attended by over one hundred women; more than three hundred participated in the second.

rather than a process through which some changes in attitudes and perspectives take place.

3. A substantial number of the forum participants expressed a feeling of confusion concerning the goals which our society has for women.

4. A number of women complained that their higher education to date had not provided the self-understanding and confidence necessary to set their own standards.

5. Women said they find themselves living in a child-centered culture, spending their time trying to keep young and evaluating themselves in terms of a "multitude of magazine and newspaper articles."

Achievement to date

An exploratory study of the need for continuing education for women was accomplished by means of a questionnaire which was distributed to the membership of well-established women's organizations in the Kansas City area.[2] The questionnaire and the segment of the population contacted were similar in many ways to those used in studies at Michigan State University and the University of Wisconsin. The questionnaire contained sections focusing on reasons for wanting to continue education, plans and needs for continuing education, interest in noncredit courses, and interest in seeking an advanced degree or completing a degree.

Data[3] obtained from the analysis of this questionnaire has been utilized in the design of two experimental noncredit courses to be offered in the fall of 1962 and as a basis for planning the next phase of our experimentation. The two noncredit courses are Art in the Context of History and The Exploration of the

[2] The leaders of these organizations were invited to a group meeting prior to the distribution of the questionnaire. This meeting provided an opportunity to discuss the general purpose of the project and to secure a basis for future cooperation with these groups. Organizations cooperating with the project are: American Association of University Women, Athenaeum, Delta Gamma Alumnae, Junior League, League of Women Voters, Leawood Women's Club, Council of Jewish Women, and Young Matrons. Twenty-five percent of 3,939 members of these organizations responded, thus making 968 questionnaires available for analysis.

[3] A report of the findings from this questionnaire is being prepared and should be available within the next few months.

Universe (based on a program of reading and discussion developed by the American Foundation for Continuing Education). These courses are being offered to meet the *most frequent request* of questionnaire respondents, which was for a course in art, and the *least frequent request*, which was for a course in science. All of the women responding to the questionnaire will receive pre-enrollment materials.

Plans are underway to evaluate these experimental courses in terms of motivations for enrollment, expectations and preconceived ideas regarding benefits to be derived from the courses, suggestions for altering them, and the organization of other non-credit courses for women.

Problems

We have learned from a preliminary analysis of the questionnaire, from the recorded group discussions held in connection with the research forums, and from individual women that there is a need for a program to close the "gap" for a substantial number of women who say they hope to continue their education but have no plans to do so.[4]

Our intention is to create on campus an experimental milieu—tentatively called a Women's Education Center—where women seeking to continue their education can have informal contact with their peers and selected faculty fellows in a specially designed academic setting. We want to try out the notion of Margaret Mead and others that peer influence is likely to be just as important in motivating this group of women to educational commitment as it is in the undergraduate and graduate student cultures. We are presently seeking support for this endeavor and for the related services and programs which our preliminary work indicates should be a part of such a center. Finally, we are concerned about the undergraduate women on our campus and hope to develop a way of making them aware of the issues and problems related to continuing education of women.

[4] Seventy percent of questionnaire respondents say they hope to continue their education, whereas only 17 percent say they have plans to do so.

REMARKS IN ELABORATION
OF WORKING PAPER

MISS BERRY: We have been creating a greater climate of interest than we may be able to handle. Our pilot survey led to two experimental courses: one in the arts and one in science. The one in the arts is filled, but it is questionnable whether we are going to be able to give the one in science. Now the pilot survey has suggested some other things. Perhaps most striking is the number of people who say almost promiscuously that they would like to continue their education but that they do not have plans to do so.

There are some fascinating things to be discovered about what happens when you expose women who say they are interested in continuing education but have no specific plans to come back to school to an experimental, almost contrived, milieu of some non-credit courses, some counseling services, and some contact with what I'm tentatively calling faculty fellows, that is, people who might be released from some teaching to be available in our center to talk informally with these women. It is my feeling that one of the things we have discovered is the variety of needs in this continuing education. I have mentioned counseling; I have mentioned the credit courses; I have mentioned the need to continue research. How these are going to fit in administratively or if they must be established on a separate basis are some of the questions that should be raised.

MRS. MERRY: Thank you. Now I would like to ask Helen Marston, director of the Program for the Retraining in Mathematics of College Graduate Women at Rutgers, for a description of their program.

[Mrs. Marston's comments follow her working paper.]

RUTGERS—THE STATE UNIVERSITY

Ford Foundation Program
for the Retraining in Mathematics
of College Graduate Women

Helen M. Marston, *director*

THE PROGRAM WAS STARTED because of the current shortage of mathematics teachers and mathematically trained personnel in all fields. The philosophy of the program is that college graduate women who have raised families and are no longer needed full time in the home are anxious to get into, or get back into, professional work, and that in order to do this they need retraining and need help. As a group, these women are probably more capable, more mature, and more stable than the average woman in the labor market today and have a valuable contribution to make which, especially at this time of need for more workers, more teachers, more scientists and mathematicians, should not be disregarded.

This program aims to demonstrate that the needs of women and the needs of society can be very happily met in programs of this type. If our society is to reap the full benefit of the education and talents of its bright women, then similar opportunities should be made available to women in other areas, both educational and geographical.

We believe that this program is unique in each of the following ways: It was preceded by a survey in which over 21,000 college graduate women, 214 industries, and 345 schools and colleges in our area (ten counties—the approximate commuting area to Newark and New Brunswick) were reached and questioned so that the program might meet the needs of all in the area in the best way possible. It is limited in its academic scope to one subject—mathematics. It is strictly vocationally oriented. The courses have been designed for women and are given at hours set for their convenience. The women study with others like themselves—just as old, just as rusty, equally diffident, and similarly motivated. Our program provides vocational guidance, academic guidance, courses, often the money for the courses, and, finally, the placement service.

Our immediate goal is so specific—namely, to get women with ability and a background of education in mathematics to go through whatever retraining is necessary for a job and then to get a job—that our achievements can be pretty well measured by counting heads. As of mid-June, nineteen heads are in full view and easy to count; another ten, roughly, are a bit obscured for one reason or another (substitute teaching is temporary; nursery school teaching is not really our achievement). Since the program has completed only three semesters, most of those who have enrolled are still in the retraining stage.

Insofar as we claim to have been successful, however, the claim is based on the types of jobs obtained, the generally high caliber of the companies that the women now in industry are working for, and the fact that nearly every woman who has enrolled in our program and has considered herself ready for a job has been placed—to date both happily and satisfactorily placed. Adjustments in the homes of these women have been made apparently with relative ease and considerable skill, thanks in part to the retraining period, which provided a bridge from housewife status to that of full-time professional employee. This kind of success, even though on a small scale, does much to give other women the confidence and courage that it takes to get back into studying and professional work, and it also does much to promote the hiring of mature women. Thus far we have had no success in placing people in part-time jobs, but the resistance to the part-time worker, we believe, is beginning to break down.

Our main problem is not enough candidates. A good class should have at least ten people in it; hence we should have at least a hundred candidates per semester, properly distributed, and thus far we have started each of our three semesters with only 53 candidates.

This may be partly due to our program's being young and as yet little known, but mathematics has never been a popular subject with women. On a six-college sample, the percent of graduates who majored in mathematics each year from 1930 to 1960 was very small, averaging about 3 percent, and did not increase during this period. (It is beginning to increase now, I believe.) Were we to run a program for the Retraining in English of College Graduate Women, we would be flooded with candidates but would have difficulty placing them.

Geographically, we are not ideally located. Our candidates come from approximately fifty miles south of New Brunswick to about fifty miles north of Newark, and in New Jersey all roads do not lead to Newark and New Brunswick, and when you do get there, there is no place to park. Dropout rate will probably always be high: husbands are transferred, children get sick, cars break down, and home responsibilities often have a way of just piling up.

REMARKS IN ELABORATION OF WORKING PAPER

MRS. MARSTON: Our program is different in one respect from what we have spoken about at this meeting. It is not really a program in continuing education, but in retraining for jobs. We serve both the needs of society and the plight of women, and to date have been equally successful, I think, in both. We have had eighteen people placed as of last June, and our program has had great acceptance from business firms. Systems Development Corporation was so interested in our program that they wanted to help with the courses in some way. They have invited us to visit for a day's orientation. Educational Testing Service has said that they are so pleased with the one woman they got and asked for another; they will even give her time off for study if she needs it. From the women's point of view we feel that we have been at least as successful. We mailed a short questionnaire to those who have gotten jobs primarily through our program, and the response was unanimously one of happiness with the job. Without exception, they all claimed that the adjustment in the home had been good. There was a spirit of cooperation in the home; the children took on responsibilities that they had not had before. There was a brand new spirit in the home, a new interest both in the mother's education and in her job, which seemed to everybody a very healthy, if a little surprising, thing.

As for number of students, I was a little misleading, I think, in my paper. We offer five courses, and because of our geographical spread, we offer these courses both in Newark and New Brunswick, which makes ten courses. This is why I said we should have at least a hundred people formally distributed for this, and we don't. I will not say that we have been disappointed by the numbers we have. When we did our survey in 1959–60, nothing in the response led us to think we would have even this many. It is not surprising that there are few when you think of the many qualifications that are necessary—the woman must have her children in school, she must be interested in retraining and in going back to work, she must be willing to give the time for retraining and must have mathematical ability. Since that survey, we have done quite a bit of study on census statistics and on college figures. Of course, there are various factors to take into account, but from 1930 to 1960 under 3 percent of women college graduates were mathematics majors. Of course we do not require that they be mathematics majors, but our research showed that interest in mathematics was also very slow during those years. A woman came into my office the other day and identifying herself as a graduate of 1938 from Smith, she said, "I got 800 on my College Board math test, but I have never taken a college math course." She smiled and added, "You know, it just wasn't the thing to do then."

What will become of the program? The way I envision it now is that it can be easily incorporated into the structure of Rutgers University. There are two aspects of this program that are different. First of all, it is given in the morning hours for the convenience of the women with school-age children. If we gave these courses in the evenings we would get an entirely new population of people who are now working. The other difference, and this applies only to two of the five courses, is that the courses really are designed for the returner. We have one course called "Review: College Freshman—Sophomore Mathematics," which is for people who have been out of school about twenty years. This course is designed to cover the material of calculus 1, calculus 2, and college algebra. The students can review and update their mathematics, which is necessary whether they are going to teach or to work in industry. There is now a slightly different vocabulary, a slightly different approach, and this they learn with their review. Therefore, it isn't quite the equivalent of a normal undergraduate course. Another course, especially designed for women, was called "Background for Teaching in Mathematics." This is solely for those who want to go into teaching and is based largely on the new curriculum materials now given in the schools. The course acts as a review and gives the new teaching approach. The state was very generous and allowed six credits toward methods or toward subject matter for certification for this course. Our other courses are computer programming, calculus, and introductory statistics.

Mrs. Merry: Now, let's hear what Esther Raushenbush is doing as director of the Center for Continuing Education at Sarah Lawrence.

[Mrs. Raushenbush's comments follow her working paper.]

SARAH LAWRENCE COLLEGE

The Center for Continuing Education

Esther Raushenbush, *director*

This program is instituted to provide educational advice and to assist in educational planning for:

1. Women whose college education was interrupted before they completed their undergraduate studies and who now wish to resume study for the bachelor of arts degree.

2. Women who have a bachelor of arts degree and wish to study for an advanced degree.

Educational advice and planning

Programs appropriate to undergraduates of college age are sometimes not suitable for individuals who have years and experience to bring to their education and whose purposes are already defined. It is a function of the center to help women who wish to resume their college education make plans appropriate to their purposes, and it seeks to help them find ways in which they may pursue their studies. Such planning may involve study at Sarah Lawrence College, study at other institutions, or special plans appropriate to the individual situation.

The staff of the center interviews prospective students and discusses with them possible plans for study. We do not have a program of vocational counseling although we do, of course, discuss the educational requirements for professional or other work women wish to undertake. The individuals this center can serve best are those who know why they want to return to study and what they would like to do after finishing the degree. We try to help them find ways by which their educational objectives can be accomplished in this community. We are limiting ourselves to work with people within commuting distance of this college, who can study in institutions within commuting distance of their homes.

For undergraduate students for whom study at Sarah Lawrence College seems indicated, the college provides several continuing education courses especially organized for persons resuming an interrupted education. These are courses offered for full college credit, taught by members of the Sarah Lawrence College faculty, and paralleling courses offered in the regular undergraduate program. They may be taken only for credit and are not open to auditors or to listeners. Students returning to study after an absence who wish to work at Sarah Lawrence College enter through one of these continuing education courses as non-matriculated students. These courses serve as a guide to the student, helping her determine whether she is ready to undertake work for the degree again; they serve as a guide to the college in deciding whether to accept the student as a degree candidate. After a semester in such a course, a student may apply to matriculate as a degree candidate and if she is accepted may enter any course in the college appropriate to her plans. Degree programs for such students are planned individually, as are our regular undergraduate programs, and in the planning we take into account the student's previous study, her intervening experience, and her present plans and expectations. If her plans call for some work not offered at the college, arrangements will be made for her to take individual courses elsewhere in the metropolitan area for which credit may be transferred to Sarah Lawrence College.

The center is able to provide information about other colleges and other institutions of higher education throughout Westchester County and in areas within commuting distance. If indications are that an individual should study at one of these institutions, the staff of the center tries to facilitate these plans by providing information and by consulting with officers of such institutions when necessary. Arrangements for independent study or other special programs will be developed as they are required to meet the needs of individual students.

In the case of prospective students who already have the bachelor's degree and who wish to undertake graduate or professional study, the staff of the center will discuss the appropriateness for graduate study of their undergraduate programs and ways in which their preparation may be supplemented if necessary. Sarah Lawrence College offers a program of graduate study leading to the master of arts degree, and students for whom that program is appropriate will be recommended for consideration to the Graduate Studies Committee of the college. The staff of the center will advise individuals about other graduate studies programs available to them.

While the center also wishes to serve women now ready to undertake full-time study, it is organized primarily for the woman who is occupied with her family and who is not now prepared to undertake full-time study, who must study within a short distance of her home, and whose plans for study and classes must take her home responsibilities into account. These will typically be part-time students.

The two most important issues to be dealt with in our program are these:

1. To help prospective students decide whether to resume study at this time, to set reasonable goals, and to determine the amount of time they can spend in order to do work of high quality and carry on their family activities.
2. To make as flexible and useful plans as we can with our institution and other institutions for this portion of the population. This means trying to arrange for part-time study in programs that typically call for full-time study and finding ways of freeing these students from some undergraduate requirements that are not as appropriate for them as they might be for the typical college undergraduate. How successful such efforts will be remains to be seen, but it is our view that the best way to develop the talents of able and mature women who need to complete their education is to consider which programs organized with the usual student in mind are appropriate for them and which, if they are to serve these individuals best, need to allow for exceptions or new planning.

The present and the immediate future

This is a new center. We had originally planned to open it this September, but when the prospective opening was announced last January a large number of women said they wanted to make plans for the coming fall and would like to get help in such planning. We opened temporary offices and have been interviewing individuals and exploring possibilities for study for them. A number of women will enter the Sarah Lawrence program, and a number will enter programs elsewhere. This fall the center will undertake a research program to discover the needs for further education of women in this community.

REMARKS IN ELABORATION
OF WORKING PAPER

MRS. RAUSHENBUSH: I want to make just two points about our program. It is a very small program that rather matches both the nature and size of our college. I especially want to stress this because it seems to me that the really exciting thing about setting up a series of new educational programs of this kind is that they can be as varied as the institutions that they are related to. The programs represented here are a very good illustration of that. Our college is a small college that has had a great deal of experience in making individual plans for students. The kind of program that has been set up is appropriate to it, and we had no roadblocks in our way as far as our own institution was concerned. In addition, the climate was favorable. We have gained considerable experience in planning with individual people whose needs differ one from the other.

This program really has two parts to it. One part is connected with our college; it belongs inside the program of the college. The program will admit this year, for example, about thirty women to study in two courses that have been planned especially for them. These two groups will be by themselves, not with the other undergraduates, and these women all want to go on to take a bachelor's degree. I think it is a good idea for a program, especially a small one, to be quite sure about what it will do and what it will not do. I think it is important for a program like this not to try to be all things to all men, and ours is quite sharply defined. All the people are candidates or want to be candidates for the bachelor's degree. All of them must have had at least one year of college. All other types of people who need and want education are important, too, but these are the ones with whom we are going to deal. Women entering these courses have not formally applied for matriculation, but the courses are five-point credit courses and can be taken only for credit. A woman may take one of these courses and decide at the end of the semester or at the end of the year whether to apply for matriculation. Once she applies for matriculation and is accepted, she then becomes a regular degree candidate in the college and takes whatever courses are appropriate for her. The courses in our program serve as a kind of bridge into the college. They give the student a chance to discover whether she really wants to study and really wants to go ahead for a degree. She is in a congenial group of people with similar objectives. By the end of the course, she has a basis for decision, and we know whether she will be an appropriate candidate for a degree. It is important that these courses be given on a level that is the same as those given for the undergraduates.

The second part of our program is advice and counsel for women who should be going somewhere else for courses our college does not offer. We happen to be so situated that we can serve a great many people by giving them advice about many types of institutions in the metropolitan area. For me, one of the most interesting aspects of this part of the program is that we are trying to break through some of the roadblocks that other people have set up.

Thus far we have had some successes and some failures in this program. For instance, most colleges do not allow their students to take their final year on another campus. A student must get his last thirty points from the college that will grant his degree. Thus far, two very respectable institutions have agreed to allow women to take their final year with us, and they will still award degrees to them. On the other hand, I have tried very hard to get a very able person to be allowed to take a performing arts program in our own college because we have a good one. This young woman had been a dance major at the University of Wisconsin. She had had three years with them, and I felt that we could work out her last year in collaboration with the University of Wisconsin and that she could be granted a Wisconsin degree, but they were not willing to do this. Another woman was not allowed to enter a liberal arts program in one of our city colleges because twenty-five years ago she had not taken the college preparatory course when she was in high school. She had to go to business school and take packaging, distribution, and merchandising, although what she really wanted to do was learn how to teach blind children. She has very bad eyesight herself and, as a braille expert, would be an excellent teacher.

Mrs. Merry: I think you all recognize that one of the fascinating things about these programs is that they differ, and they differ in terms of the institutions in which they are housed and the people who are directing them. Still a different type is

houses at Radcliffe. We are providing, in a way, models of women who are combining their scholarly and domestic activities. And one of the undergraduates said to me the other day after she had finished her honors thesis and had received highest honors, "You know, along about March I almost bogged down with my study. Then I got to talking with one of the people at the institute tea and somehow regained my perspective. Instead of quitting, I went ahead because she showed me that maybe sometime my degree might come in handy." I won't suggest this as a proper motivation, but the model idea and the incorporation of these people into an undergraduate community does far more than anything we can do by preaching to the young people. The example is far better than the precept.

And finally, I would ask for your suggestions and comments on the problem of counseling. In addition to the members of the institute or, as we call them, the associate scholars and affiliate scholars, who are medical people refurbishing their medical training preparatory for private practice, we have had about one hundred fifty to two hundred women coming to talk with our staff psychologist about plans for going back to work or for taking further training. Besides workshop sessions, our psychologist assigned readings and led them through a series of discussions trying to investigate some alternative possibilities. From her comments and her reports, certain characteristics of these women have emerged. Our particular problem is the transient nature of the American woman as she follows her husband from job assignment to job assignment. People become somewhat disassociated from their collegiate connections and in a new community and do not know where to turn for the kind of serious-minded advice they need.

The lack of self-confidence is an outstanding characteristic, not only of people who have come seeking advice on whether to go back to school, but also of the women who have Ph.D.'s and have had considerable experience in the field but have been away from their own profession for some years and who simply do not know where to go. They have lost a sense of professional purpose that is extremely important to their accomplishment.

These are some of the characteristics that we have found.

We will be carrying on some research at the institute; we have received one grant specifically for research and have some funds from our budget for this.

MRS. MERRY: Still another plan is that of the American Association of University Women, and Pauline Tompkins, the general director of the AAUW, will share some of her observations of this plan with us.

[Miss Tompkins's comments follow her working paper.]

AMERICAN ASSOCIATION OF UNIVERSITY
WOMEN EDUCATIONAL FOUNDATION

College Faculty Program

Pauline Tompkins, *general director*

THE OBJECTIVE of the College Faculty Program of the American Association of University Women Educational Foundation is to increase the resources of qualified personnel for higher education. The urgency of national need for qualified faculty in colleges and universities is great. Young people are turning to college careers in greater numbers than before, but there are not enough of them nor can they be prepared fast enough to meet the need. The AAUW program is based on the assumption that there are a great many able and interested women college graduates in their middle years who, with further education, would make excellent career faculty.

For that reason, and solely to augment the supply of faculty members, the Educational Foundation sought financial support for a three-year demonstration program in eleven Southern states. The foundation has been fortunate in receiving a grant of $225,000 from the Rockefeller Brothers Fund for that purpose. The program is unique in its single mindedness: to increase the supply of qualified college faculty. It is unusual in that it is willing to work with high ability women who may have earned no more than a bachelor's degree and to offer them tuition and fees for full-time study toward an advanced degree (candidates who have earned doctorates are also eligible) and a small stipend to cover additional expenses. This support is for one year only. It gives the awardee a chance to re-enter academic life under favorable conditions. She can concentrate on her studies so that by the end of the year she will have demonstrated to the graduate school her ability to compete fully with other students, especially for support for completion of her graduate degrees and for recommendations for faculty positions. The graduate school which accepts the student receives a small cost-of-education subsidy.

One of the responsibilities assumed by the AAUW Educational Foundation is to counsel applicants to the program, whether eligible or not, as well as the awardees. Assistance in placement will also be given wherever possible.

As of the autumn of 1962, eighteen able women will be in full-time study at thirteen Southern graduate schools within commuting distance of their residences. They will be studying in such different fields as mathematics, psychology, plant pathology, English, and home economics. One is doing postdoctoral study, thirteen are master's degree candidates and four are seeking the doctorate. They range in age from thirty-four to fifty; sixteen are married, and two are single.

The program has significance for the whole country, though financial support is given for a demonstration program in only eleven Southern states. After six months of operation, it is already clear that this program will present new information about the problems of re-entering formal education after a long absence, and statements of the need for such a program have been received from other parts of the country. Many requests have come from mature, able, and available women who have almost completed their graduate education but who lack necessary financing to finish and whose education must be subsidized if they are to become career faculty members.

The College Faculty Program has already demonstrated the need of college women for information about appropriate second careers and for help in selecting and preparing for them. The graduate schools and their departments have been most co-operative and cordial in joining in the demonstration. We anticipate that new evidence on which future admissions can be based will emerge from this experience.

REMARKS IN ELABORATION OF WORKING PAPER

Miss Tompkins: AAUW's Educational Foundation Program is unique in the sense that its single purpose is to prepare mature college women for going into college level work either in research, in teaching, or in administration. To the best of our knowledge there is no other program that has joined us in doing this exclusively. It is our feeling that what we need to do is to identify women who have not been actively engaged in academic work at a graduate level for some years and to make it possible, through rather modest grants, for them to resume their education and have their fees taken care of for one year. At the end of that time some may be ready to go into college teaching, whereas others should have proved to the institutions in which they are studying that they are able to compete successfully with the other graduate students. We are also unique in that we are not a college but rather are acting as a kind of middleman or perhaps I should say a midwife; we are unique in that we are delivering mature women to institutions.

Dr. Blackwell made a comment about the resistance which some faculties of higher institutions may express toward admitting older women into graduate programs. Before we received our grant from the Rockefeller Brothers Fund, we investigated whether such a program could find institutions who would be willing to cooperate and accept mature women. We visited a number of institutions in the South which are included in the program and talked to college and university presidents, deans of graduate schools, and college faculty counsels. I concluded that we would meet with no resistance whatsoever on the part of those with whom we talked, and our experience has borne this out.

Our first step after making an award is to get in touch with the college or university graduate school to find out if our assessment of the candidate's qualifications meet with the policy of the institution. In every instance except one there was no question whatsoever; all were admitted. In the case of the one who was discouraged, the reason was because she would have to commute one hundred miles a day, and the institution itself felt that this was too much. We had not realized the transportation problem was as grave as it was.

We still have a number of problems that we are concerned with. We have found that our program is doing something we had not intended that it would do; it is discriminating against single women. The single woman who has the sole responsibility for earning her living has more difficulty in entering our program than the married woman who does not have a job. This problem has distressed us very much, and we have yet to come to grips with it. We also find that the need for financial aid is much greater than the amount we have to give, with the result that we are going to have to reduce the total number of awards to ensure that the candidates we choose will have the necessary funds.

My concluding point is a bit peripheral to the others, but related. A problem still to be determined is what will happen to these women after they have qualified for college teaching. Are they going to be accepted? The institutions have accepted them as students; we do not expect these same institutions to take them on their faculty but will other institutions accept them? This is a question that we all must consider, for as you know, there is a great deal of discrimination still practiced in our colleges and universities in regard to the employment of women, their promotion on faculties, their tenure, and their salaries.

Mrs. Merry: Our next speaker will be Mrs. Vera Schletzer, codirector of the Minnesota Plan.

[Mrs. Schletzer's comments follow her working paper.]

UNIVERSITY OF MINNESOTA

The Minnesota Plan

Vera Schletzer, *codirector*

THE MINNESOTA PLAN was formally established at the University of Minnesota in June 1960 with the assistance of a grant of $110,000 from the Carnegie Corporation of New York for its first three years of operation. Its two objectives are: first, to return to the nation's paid and unpaid manpower pool a group of intelligent, educated women whose talents might otherwise be underused during their mature years; and second, to increase the personal happiness of many women by exposing them to new interests, by helping them to find new objectives, and by making the goals of the more distant future an integral part of their present lives. The Minnesota Plan is neither a college nor a curriculum nor a superinstitution. It is a facilitating and coordinating agency which aims to explore, exploit, and explain the available resources of the university to women and, conversely, to influence the university so that its facilities are more readily available for efficient, effective use by women.

The objectives of a program for the continuing education of already mature women necessitate different methods than those for young adult women. The mature woman who feels that she is not using her abilities to their fullest extent needs immediate and individualized help. She does not have a high school counselor to aid her in choosing the "right" college and "right" curriculum. She is hesitant to approach a staff member to ask which courses are appropriate to bring her "rusty" degree or major up to date. She may not want to resume a previous career and needs help in determining a new direction. Generally, she needs support, information, and assurance that there is a sympathetic and dignified means of approach to the university or the world of work. The personnel of the Minnesota Plan try to expedite this return in many ways: by counseling, referrals to other persons on and off campus, job placement, liberal arts seminars designed especially for mature women, neighborhood seminars, scholarships, and special programs designed to meet specific needs—whether they be for information on schools of tomorrow or lectures on how to study. It has been our experience that many offerings have unexpected benefits. For instance, a newsletter distributed for information purposes often has motivational results.

The young adult woman has different needs from those of mature women although she may not be aware of them. With information in all fields expanding at such a rapid rate, she needs to plan ahead realistically. Although some undergraduates have had individual help from the Minnesota Plan personnel, we feel that much can be done in group situations. Part of our function is to educate and indoctrinate the personnel of the university who already have a responsibility for these students. Several of our "rusty" ladies report that the concern they felt twenty years ago for their own futures was met with cavalier treatment on the part of their advisers; our hope is to prevent this today.

To a great extent the uniqueness of the Minnesota Plan lies in the fact that it has been a pioneer and a leader in the concept of women's continuing education, although it is sometimes difficult to be a leader when you are still exploring uncharted territory. Also, the attitudes and facilities of a large state university in a metropolitan center provide opportunities that differ from those possible in other types of institutions in other locations. The University of Minnesota provides a climate that is receptive to innovation and experimentation.

The outstanding accomplishments of the Minnesota Plan for the Continuing Education of Women are, of course, the enrollment in the plan of almost seven hundred mature women and their individual success stories, along with over one hundred young women who have come to us for counseling about their futures. The interest and active support of already overburdened faculty must rank among our greatest achievements. The great amount of publicity, mostly unsolicited, that the program has received is another important accomplishment, for it indicates a general and growing concern with the problem of continuing education. During the past year, our staff members have been asked to address sixty-nine groups. The far-reaching and long-term effects of these printed and spoken words are difficult to evaluate.

Our biggest problem is to get young women who are undergraduates to concern themselves with planning for continuing education. We have not yet reached faculty advisers in a way that satisfies us, and we were disappointed that the undergraduate seminar failed to attract adequate registration in its second year. Specific changes in university procedures that would be helpful are: (1) credit by examination in the social sciences, as we now have in mathematics and languages, (2) courses given during daytime hours but only once a week, as they are in the evening extension classes, and (3) elimination of certain fees for services used by the resident undergraduate but not the part-time mature student. Most important, we need the time and the staff to do research on the many problems connected with the continuing education of women.

REMARKS IN ELABORATION
OF WORKING PAPER

MRS. SCHLETZER: From the great interest and enthusiasm with which women have approached the Minnesota Plan, you can see that we do not have to coerce women into coming back to school. We have to make the existing resources of the university available to them, and once they are available, the women will take advantage of them. We have had approximately 882 women come to us for help in using our resources. With the exception of the liberal arts seminars, and our counseling and guidance programs, we have added nothing new to the University of Minnesota. Perhaps many of you, too, have a flexible program available at your institutions but have not let the public know about it.

We do not screen applicants to the Minnesota Plan; one simply has to be a resident of the state and feel that she can benefit from the University of Minnesota to join the plan. Thus we have had some women who may have joined it by mistake. In

May of this year we sent a follow-up questionnaire to 471 women who had joined the plan prior to January. We asked how many had actually taken courses, whether they were daytime courses at the university, daytime courses elsewhere, extension division seminars, regularly scheduled evening classes, correspondence courses, or any college level work. Sixty-four percent, or 302 women, returned their questionnaires. I've asked several people to guess the percentage of women who have actually taken college level work since joining the plan, and I consistently got 20 percent as an estimate. Actually 72 percent of those answering have taken college level courses, and another 15 percent plan to start within this next year. Only 6 percent of the women answering have not taken courses, are not working, and have no firm plans to do so in the near future. I think this is evidence of the need and the seriousness of the women coming to us.

Mrs. Merry: Unfortunately, Mr. Bernard Stern, associate director of the School of General Studies at Brooklyn College, could not join us tonight, but the description of the program at Brooklyn College will reveal an interesting and unique approach to the continuing education of men as well as of women.

BROOKLYN COLLEGE

Special Baccalaureate Degree Program for Adults

Bernard H. Stern, *associate director, School of General Studies*

THE SPECIAL BACCALAUREATE DEGREE Program for Adults at Brooklyn College was established in 1953 as an experimental effort to meet the following objections of adults to formal degree study:

1. We already know from life experience much of what you require us to study.
2. We can go much faster than youngsters in a college curriculum.
3. We are treated like children in the classroom; we would do better if taught on an adult level.

The program has successfully solved these problems by providing for academic credit for life experience, accelerating adults by tutorial service and independent study, and establishing basic seminars in the four divisions of knowledge equivalent to the general education courses of the first two years of college, followed by advanced seminars which achieve integration and depth intellectually superior to the ordinary senior year.

The program differs from other adult projects in these respects:

1. It leads to a standard, regularly accredited, bachelor of arts or bachelor of science degree, fully recognized as valid for admission to graduate and professional schools.

2. It is possible for an adult without advanced standing who attends college only in the evening to attain the degree in about four years. If he is able to attend some day classes, the period of residence may be reduced to three years. In the regular curriculum the earning of the degree may take as long as twelve years.

3. The seminars, the core of the educational process of this program, are unique in their adult quality, their integration at a high level of scholarship, and their intellectual stimulation.

The most significant achievements of the program are that it clarifies the liberal arts value of adult experience; it prods faculty minds to think through the meaning of academic credit; it conducts research into the nature of adults as students; it establishes a relationship among life experience, intellectual acuity, emotional stability, adult motivation, personal growth, and social usefulness; and it illuminates the problem of screening procedures for college admissions. The chief problem faced by our committee has been the recruitment of teachers of adults qualified for the kind of commitment to adult education which this program requires.

Group Discussions
of Assigned Questions

On the morning of the last day of the conference, the participants divided into small groups to discuss questions prepared
for them by the Conference Steering Committee. Summaries of
these group discussions follow and include many courses of
action that universities and colleges could follow to establish,
promote, and encourage programs of continuing education for
women.

DISCUSSION GROUP 1
Leader: C. Easton Rothwell

> *With reference to the continuing education of women,
> what new administrative and program arrangements are
> needed in colleges and universities in order to improve the
> yield of guidance and counseling? What innovations in
> guidance and counseling are possible in agencies other than
> colleges and universities?*

It was the unanimous judgment of the committee that there
should be one person in the reference service of the college or
university who could serve as a focal point for continuing
education. This function should be set aside from, but related to,
the general counseling and guidance functions of the institution.

Although there are some institutions in which counseling and
guidance related to continuing education are handled solely by the
guidance service itself, the more normal arrangement would
require a referral from the person serving as the focal point to
the various branches of the college or university, to the administration, to the faculty involved in the educational program, to the
psychologists where special guidance in this area is necessary, or
if the woman is interested in research, to those concerned with
research programs.

There should be a close working relationship between counseling and guidance in each of these areas. At the same time, the person serving as the focal point for counseling and guidance should handle problems such as that posed by a young woman who indicates that she wants to get a Ph.D. in economics in order to engage in economic analysis. If the counseling and guidance person is persuaded economics is not the field in which this woman will do best, there should be some discussion of this and some special consultation with persons in economics. Through the focal point for counsel, the woman seeking a continuing education should acquire a better knowledge of the opportunities available in the college or university. Often times, ignorance rather than lack of desire has been responsible for mistakes in programming.

Some advantages can be gained by handling women in groups once they have been seen as individuals. Guidance given in groups can lead to mutual stimulation and clarification and tends to increase motivation. This is the experience of institutions, like the University of Minnesota, where this has been done.

Finally, it should be remembered that the real motivation for continuing education will be implanted during the growing-up and maturing period. This means the undergraduate years as far as college is concerned. Hence, counseling and guidance on continuing education should be extended to the undergraduate years and, in cooperation with other programs of counseling and guidance, should be geared toward the specific problems of the undergraduate.

Under any circumstances, the conditions essential to the success of a counseling and guidance program are: (1) warm support from the faculty and administration; (2) confidence on the part of the students; (3) a measure of flexibility in the educational program itself which permits some adjustment and adaptation; and (4) persons of high quality in the counseling function who are able to win faculty, administrative, and student support and confidence.

The group is aware that counseling and guidance is carried on by the Red Cross, the YWCA, the AAUW, certain industries, and certain unions. In large measure, this is precollege or pre-university counseling and should not be confused with that conducted in the educational institutions. Insofar as there is a relationship between the institutions and these agencies, a liaison should be established to prevent contradictory advising or undesirable forms of overlap. On the other hand, the kinds of counseling and guidance given by these outside agencies may afford alternative programs in continuing education that may be of great significance to women.

DISCUSSION GROUP 2

Leader: VIRGINIA SENDERS

> *Given the pressures of increasing enrollments and continuing shortages of faculty members, what active steps can educational institutions take to meet the needs for continuing education in their own communities?*

In interpreting our assignment, the members of the group decided not to attempt to solve the problems posed by enrollment pressures and faculty shortages, but to address themselves primarily to the question of the development of continuing education programs that are realistic and feasible under these probable future conditions. The group's conclusions and suggestions can be summarized under three main headings: policy, implementation, and financing.

Policy

The most important single step that can be taken by educational institutions to support continuing education is to believe in it. For years, lip service has been paid to the principle that education continues throughout life, but in actual practice, the fulfillment of adult needs is placed at the very bottom of the hierarchy of institutional responsibilities. The four-year package continues to be accepted as a norm; teaching assignments are made with no thought of the continuing education needs of the community; funds are allocated for continuing education only when all other requests have been filled; class schedules are made up and curricular requirements determined with no thought of the needs of the mature student. The junior colleges and community colleges, of course, provide the notable exception to these generalizations, and we may well look to them for leadership in the continuing education movement. Such gains as have already been made should be followed up *now*, while the movement is showing remarkable vigor across the whole country. The continuing education of women is only a part of the whole, but it is a part of such importance, a part where innovation is so relatively easy, that for the movement as a whole it may serve as the spearhead of progress.

The group felt that the American Council on Education, as the representative body of higher educational institutions in America, should issue a policy statement announcing strong and wholehearted support of the philosophy of continuing education and should encourage its member institutions to exploit old ways and seek new ways for implementing this philosophy.

Implementation

An institution truly committed to the principle of continuing education will find numerous ways of implementing its beliefs, even in the face of mounting enrollments and faculty shortages.

One of the most important and least expensive steps an institution can take is to examine its own procedures, including degree requirements, class schedules, tuition and fee structure, course prerequisites, and the like, with the needs of the mature, part-time student in mind. Inevitably, unexpected obstacles will appear. In one university, the fee structure severely penalizes the part-time student. In another, an unexpected physical education requirement prevents grandma from obtaining the coveted degree, or a required orientation course presents an absurd waste of time for a mature business man. To seek out and remove such obstacles is a real step forward in the support of continuing education.

An institution may already have taken this first important step and may feel that its offerings—its schedules, its fees, its requirements—are truly geared to the needs of the mature student. Its next job is to publicize its wares. Members of the community need to know what is available to them. They need to know that they are welcome. They need to know that others like themselves are already making use of the university's offerings. Only then will going to school for life really seem like a completely natural, normal, reasonable thing for anyone to do. Right now, public relations is an integral part of the total educational job that remains to be done, for it is largely through public relations that attitudes are shaped and expectations formed. Many of the community and junior colleges have already taken these two important steps and have established their right to serve as models for other institutions. Widespread use of available educational resources by members of the community would, of course, mean additional pressure on enrollments in an era of coming faculty shortages. Ways must be sought to use teaching resources more effectively and to exploit untapped sources of faculty personnel. Full utilization of instructional aids such as programmed learning, correspondence courses, independent study, proficiency examinations, audio-visual aids, and very large classes will lead to more effective use of faculty time and ability. But these aids must be used correctly—not in such a way that the education of masses of people becomes nothing more than the education of people *in* masses. Our goal should remain the creation of a climate conducive to the full development of each individual to his own maximum potential. The Brooklyn College program, for example, takes as its starting point the evaluation of individual accomplishments and deficiencies and seeks individual ways to accredit the accomplishments and remove the deficiencies. It succeeds in weaving adult experience into the fabric of academic progress.

To achieve such a climate will require not only the full and efficient use of faculty members in such numbers as we now have, but the discovery and exploitation of new sources of teaching personnel. For example, regulations governing faculty retirement must be constantly scrutinized to foster the continued use of the talents of wise and experienced men and women who, though they have reached some specified chronological age, may be biologically and psychologically younger than colleagues who have had fewer birthdays. And women's talents must be used more fully. There are many forms of discrimination against women on college faculties; some are overt, some covert. A few institutions quite openly state their preference for men. But women's potential professorial careers are less handicapped by such outspoken discrimination than by antinepotism regulations and by the unspoken requirement of "publish or perish." Women who are raising families, as President Clapp of Wellesley has pointed out, can readily maintain their professional knowlege and continue as effective teachers and advisers, but seldom can they add a research load to these other time- and emotion-consuming activities. To lose them as teachers or treat them as second-raters because they cannot simultaneously be wives, mothers, researchers, *and* teachers seems criminally wasteful. And instead of arbitrarily excluding faculty wives from teaching positions, we should examine their ranks for overlooked potential.

In addition to women and older faculty members, there may be an additional source of teaching personnel in the community. In industry, in government, in business, there are men (and women) who would welcome the opportunity to do some college teaching without devoting a major portion of their time to it. To some extent, such persons are already being sought out, especially by the evening colleges, but with a flexible system of individual or group tutorials combined with proficiency examinations, their abilities could be used even more fully and effectively.

Financing

More faculty members, changed schedules, better teaching aids —these will cost money. The money may come from three kinds of sources: individual tuitions and fees, private endowment and grants, and governmental aid. For a number of years, the Federal Government has been expending large sums of money for rural and agricultural education. But the United States has now become an urban society, and the urgent need at present is for the support of continuing education programs in urban centers. The General Extension Bill may be a source of funds for this purpose, and the group concurred in the hope that no unnecessary limitations would be placed on the institutions that were eligible for support under it. They should, of course, be accredited institutions, but should not be limited, for example, to public or private ones, or large or small ones.

For some time to come, private foundations may be expected to provide a substantial proportion of the funds for continuing education programs, especially those that are novel or experimental. In preparing proposals for foundations and in soliciting their support, voluntary organizations and citizens' groups might have significant contributions to make. Similarly, these same groups could help obtain legislative support and state funds for educational programs designed to meet the needs of the entire community. In general, a broader concept of the community's role in educational financing is needed.

Conclusion

Where there is a need and a real desire to meet that need, it will be met. Today there is a real need for more first-class educational offerings from the colleges and universities to the adults of their communities. The ways in which programs can be revised and supplemented are numerous, as are the possible sources of funds. Ultimately, what will determine our progress will be our policy, in the broadest meaning of that word. If we really want to do this job right, we can. The most important action we can take now is really to want.

DISCUSSION GROUP 3

Leader: SUSAN COBBS

> *What are the needed innovations in colleges and universities that would enable them to maintain continuous contact with women graduates and perhaps nongraduates who are engaged in the earlier years of homemaking?*

The group felt that innovations are not needed so much as a more imaginative use of facilities already in existence. These can be directed more specifically toward maintaining contact with alumnae. Better use of existing facilities can be made in the following ways:

1. Organize counseling of women in such a way as to recognize that careers or even education may be interrupted and then resumed. It is important that such counseling be done with freshmen and sophomores as well as with upper-class women.

2. Encourage faculty members to keep careful records of majors and their subsequent activities. This can be one of the most effective lines of communication between alumna and institution.

3. Publicize in the alumni bulletins material that recognizes the concerns of women whose education or career has been interrupted. Both "precept and example" can be used.

4. Conduct an exit interview to establish a relationship with women who leave college before graduation and continue to communicate with such women through a special office or a part of the alumni office. In this way a return to academic work when the right time comes can be encouraged and facilitated.

5. Use all possible educational devices to reach beyond the institution: for example, television, alumnae seminars.

DISCUSSION GROUP 4

Leader: BROTHER LEO V. RYAN

> *What institutional reforms should be considered with reference to the increasing physical mobility of American families?*

This male-dominated, administrative-oriented group approached our question somewhat gingerly. In this report we wish to suggest some techniques which might be explored and researched in considering the special problems we face in the continuing education of women. At the same time we wish to indicate that our suggestions for study should not be interpreted as a recommendation to relaxation in the administration of existing programs, but rather these suggestions point out possibilities for the realistic adjustment of procedures to achieve desirable goals.

Our suggestions are motivated by several considerations:

1. We believe that there is need for greater administrative flexibility and administrator friendliness—administrative flexibility toward highly rigid regulations as they generally exist and administrator friendliness toward highly motivated persons as they exist, even if they do not conform to neat, administrative categories.

2. We believe that traditionalism, which has been identified with educational institutions and which was rooted in the circumstances and spirit of an earlier time, was more appropriate to a time in which our society was less mobile. These traditions should be reviewed in the light of a changing society and of the greater mobility of our people.

3. We are essentially discussing undergraduate education, but not necessarily limiting our consideration to this area.

4. We question whether mobility of population and, therefore, study in several institutions really contributes to an eroding of the value of a degree. We wonder if this argument might suggest the need to restructure various degree programs, to rebuild the degree programs rather than to attempt to patch the present programs.

Specific suggestions offered by our discussion group were the following:

1. Review the present regulation in the acceptance and transfer of credits.

2. Increase the possibilities for independent study, reading, and research.

3. Increase the opportunities for students to qualify for credits by examination.

4. Liberalize requirements for advanced standing in programs of study by methods other than credit through examination.

5. Waiver prerequisites when the candidate can demonstrate equivalent or more than equivalent preparation and experience.

6. Give special consideration to an earlier participation in honors programs and seminars.

7. Give greater weight to experience and establish an educational equivalency for experience.

8. Conduct research into the methods, procedures, and substance of credit transfer between and among institutions.

9. Put less emphasis on credits and greater emphasis on educational achievement and accomplishment.

10. Allow mature students to secure a degree through comprehensive examination in areas of learning rather than in traditional courses. Preparation can range through a variety of educational techniques.

11. Ease the transition from one type of institution to another, for example, the transition from a small liberal arts school for girls to a large, complex state university.

12. Review the entire area of certification in terms of uniform and standard certification policies. There is a need for greater coordination among existing groups and for perfecting examinations.

13. Consider wider acceptance of extramural programs.

The suggestions offered by this group have a striking resemblance to many of the ideas which appear in the Report of the Council on Inter-University Cooperation based on findings of a study and conferences financed by the Carnegie Foundation. This discussion group recommends a study of that report as a source of ideas to help solve the present need for institutional reforms resulting from the increasing mobility of American families.

DISCUSSION GROUP 5

Leader: PAUL WARD

> *Contrasted with those of men, are the differences in the life cycles of women sufficient to justify special programs and services for the continuing education of women? If yes, what are the essential variations that should be arranged in such programs and services?*

We answered the first question with a quick "Yes." As to the second question, we agreed that special counseling is needed when a woman resumes the process of education in her mature years. Programs for the continuing education of women should be publicized to encourage those who need only friendly advice and thoughtful guidance. Going beyond that, we would suggest that college vocational offices publicize any special guidance services to alumnae. Those colleges with tight exclusion policies with regard to older students should decide whether they will serve only those between the ages of eighteen and twenty-two or if they now have an additional responsibility to educate mature women. If they accept this responsibility, they should then provide certain instructional services and be flexible enough to make exceptions to the usual registration requirements and to cope with the special problems of returnees. These colleges should also take a more realistic view of what their degree means and should be willing to grant a degree to those who may not have had four years under their own instruction but who have satisfactorily fulfilled basic requirements.

Adult evening colleges and all colleges offering courses to mature women with family responsibilities should schedule classes at convenient times during the day. For example, a long seminar one day a week might be much more satisfactory than three classes per week. Those colleges and universities developing an adult program would do well to experiment with one or more introductory courses—courses designed exclusively for women returning to academic life. Such courses might be planned in consultation with students rather than by the administration or the faculty alone.

The group made the following recommendations for the education and counseling of undergraduate women: First, the vocational office should point out the problems of re-entering a career after dropping out and the possibilities (or impossibilities) for part-time work in certain careers, so that students who currently are not looking much beyond marriage are made aware of the special problems of interrupting their education or their work record. Second, the vocational office should conduct an exit interview with each dropout. Third, the faculty should be encouraged to rethink and reorganize certain undergraduate courses in view of the interrupted educational pattern of many women students.

DISCUSSION GROUP 6
Leader: CARL GRIP

> *What are the more urgent areas of research to backstop improved continuing education of women? Are there specific directives to be suggested to agencies such as colleges and universities, private and public organizations, and governmental departments at all levels?*

In carrying out the charge above, our discussion group recognized that some of the following recommendations might properly be labeled as areas for research but that, more often, the recommendations involve the more mundane tasks of assembling information or data. We suspect that there already exists a good deal of data and some studies relevant to these questions. The mandate to delineate materials needed to "backstop" improved continuing education of women was taken literally. Implicit in most of our questions are assumptions which are not questioned but for which more substantial supporting data is sought:

1. It appears that a barrier exists in the form of a fear on the part of the mature woman that she will not be able to learn as easily as she would have when she was younger. The literature on IQ development has tended to suggest this. The University of Chicago's study, on the other hand, would seem to indicate that mature women perform better in the classroom than their "college-age" counterparts. More information on this point needs to be assembled and widely disseminated so as to reach women who may be considering a return to school.

2. Related to our first recommendation is the concern about the appropriateness of existing entrance and achievement tests for these women. Do these tests, with their emphasis upon substantive knowledge, blur the potential of these women to regain what may have been lost through disuse? Also, since even tests which aim primarily at abilities necessarily involve substantive material, do they thus underestimate the potential of these women as earlier forms of IQ tests were found to discriminate against city-bred children who had never seen cows?

3. More information is needed about the career patterns and choices of women who continue their education. What relationship is there to the career expectations expressed when they were in high school or when they previously attended college? To what extent is the resumption of education a consequence of changes in career choices? What problems are involved in such changes? Are there discernible trends for this group? (We are mindful, for instance, of some cases which were cited of women leaving quite lucrative jobs to take what they considered to be more challenging positions.)

4. What is the placement picture? Effective counseling with these women must await better and more extensive data on the types of jobs that are or will be available to women.

5. In instances where women have requisite skills and sex discrimination does not bar them from particular jobs, the availability of the jobs to women or, conversely, the tendency for women to fill the positions may depend upon special arrangements not directly related to the performance of the skill. Thus some women will be available for part-time employment who could not accept full-time employment. Cultural expectations seem to demand that when the husband or children are ill the wife takes charge, while the converse is not true. What are the unique demands made upon a married woman which affects her availability for employment? To what extent do these bar her from appropriate employment and deprive the nation of her talents? What changes can be made in employment patterns (hours, physical conditions) to alleviate this problem?

6. What are the implications for family life when the woman returns to school or takes employment? What is the effect upon her husband and children?

7. What types of financial assistance are needed to make continuing education available? What other material problems are involved for women going back to school?

8. The usual college curriculum and the patterns in which it is made available have been designed for full-time undergraduates just out of high school or, in some instances, for a somewhat amorphous evening school population. Are there other forms of

educational opportunities or other patterns or media which might be employed?

9. Related to the questions concerning career choices is lack of information about the incentives and motives of women who return to school. For instance, we have phrased several of these recommendations in terms of jobs. How many women who return to school are doing so for enrichment without intending later to seek employment? Our concern to provide opportunities for employment to women and to make available to the nation the skills of these women is already apparent. We should also be concerned with the improvement of continuing education in a non-vocational sense.

10. The growing number and variety of special programs in continuing education is gratifying. The usefulness of information about these programs to other institutions will be greatly enhanced if follow-up studies are made. We urge the institutions which have existing programs to carefully evaluate them, their patterns, and the participants and to make this information available.

DISCUSSION GROUP 7
Leader: ROYCE PITKIN

> *What are the needed innovations in campus experiences that would enable women students to better understand the multiple roles they will play in later life?*

The general climate of the campus should be characterized by recognition on the part of the administration, the faculty, and student advisers of woman's specific role and educational needs. Our group recommends the establishment of a center of responsibility on each campus for the creation of the desired climate. It is felt that unless some person or agency serves as such a center the creation of the desired climate is likely to be bypassed because of the pressures of other interests.

The group recommends that institutional regulations be modified wherever necessary to make it easier for women to complete their interrupted education and to permit the employment of women as faculty members on a part-time basis, and that nepotism rules be modified so that women may be employed by the same institution as their husbands.

The group urges that the influence of models on the lives of students be recognized by helping younger students get acquainted with women faculty members who carry multiple roles, by permitting mature women to participate in undergraduate courses, by inviting to the campus as speakers and consultants women who are known to carry a variety of roles and who represent wide experiences. The group agreed that courses for undergraduate women should be planned to include experiences outside the classroom and even outside the campus which would demonstrate the varying roles of women and that provision be made for the discussion and interpretation of these experiences; that established courses should incorporate discussions of the roles women perform and that these discussions be supplemented by use of the film, television, literature, and drama.

Campus services should include those provided by counselors who are oriented to the specific problems of women as well as counseling for dropouts. The group felt that there was a special opportunity for counseling through the placement services. It was pointed out that vocational planning programs should be tempered with consideration of women's unique lives. The group recommends that information be designed to interpret to prospective college students, their parents, and high school counselors the kind of education needed for women in their multiple roles and that this information be disseminated through pamphlets, alumni journals, admissions offices, and speakers.

The final recommendation was that studies should be made of what women students actually think at various stages in their college careers about the roles of women. Such studies may reveal that women students are already giving a great deal of thought to the kinds of lives they are likely to lead, or they may reveal quite the opposite. It is also quite possible that their views change markedly as they move through college.

DISCUSSION GROUP 8
Leader: ERWIN STEINBERG

> *Given such exemplary programs for the continuing educa-*
> *tion of women as those now being sponsored by the report-*
> *ing institutions, what additional types of programs or serv-*
> *ices would enrich the current experimentation? In short,*
> *are there experimental ideas that have been overlooked?*

Our group felt that the following types of programs or services should be explored:

1. New channels and devices need to be developed to disseminate information about the need for continuing education for women and about programs of continuing education. The newsletter, *Women's Education,* of the American Association of University Women is excellent, but both the public and the colleges need additional sources of information.

2. Special counseling programs for women need to be developed and then introduced into the schools and colleges.

3. Facilities and services already available, such as extension programs, evening schools, the program to make mathematics teachers out of retired naval officers, and counseling bureaus, need to be adapted to continuing education for women.

4. Urban, area, state, or regional centers should be established to coordinate the facilities of colleges and universities, museums, and educational television stations for use in continuing education programs.

5. A policy to facilitate the transfer of college credits needs to be developed by the American Council on Education.

6. The four-year college program should be compartmentalized into two two-year programs. The educational disadvantages here are obvious, but it would be worth exploring this idea to see whether the facilitating of transferring as a result of such an organization of curricula might outweigh the disadvantages.

Resolutions of the Conference

THE FOLLOWING THREE RESOLUTIONS were adopted by unanimous vote of the conference:

Resolution Number 1

The Conference on the Continuing Education of Women, meeting at Itasca State Park, Minnesota, September 6–8, 1962, gratefully acknowledges its appreciation to the American Council on Education for sponsorship of the conference; to the Carnegie Corporation of New York for assistance that made the conference possible; to the University of Minnesota for leadership and staff assistance in the development and carrying out of the conference program; to the steering committee; to those who prepared papers, addressed the conference, and participated in the discussions at the conference sessions; and to the management and staff at Itasca State Park for the pleasant accommodations.

Resolution Number 2

The Conference on the Continuing Education of Women, meeting at Itasca State Park, Minnesota, September 6–8, 1962, under the auspices of the American Council on Education, reaffirms the significance to society of women's continuing education and of the role of American universities and colleges in such education.

In this conviction, recognizing strength in the potential diversity of the programs institutions may devise and relying on the opinion, often stated by many conferees, that this conference should lead into action, we earnestly request the president of the American Council on Education to appoint a committee charged to seek out ways in which, under the aegis of the Council, its member colleges and universities may be encouraged to originate and sustain effective programs for women's continuing education.*

* Editor's Note: During the 1962–63 academic year, responsibility within the American Council on Education for program development in the field of women's education was assigned to the Commission on Academic Affairs.

Resolution Number 3

The Conference on the Continuing Education of Women, meeting at Itasca State Park, Minnesota, September 6–8, 1962, brings to the attention of the Committee on Education of the President's Commission on the Status of Women the deliberations and ideas presented at the conference, as reported in the conference proceedings, and urges that the committee include in its report to the commission the importance of continuing education of women at all educational levels.

The Facts, the Hopes,
and the Possibilities

Margaret Culkin Banning
Author

THIS CONFERENCE will have its small niche in educational history, for never before has a national meeting been called to consider the subject which concerns us here. It has been a brave and a frank conference, its participants have made it a very distinguished one. At the conclusion of this meeting, we are certain that the need and desire for continuing education of American women is not regional but national, although it is not yet pervasive in the United States by any means. But the fires of interest have sprung up in noncontiguous areas and have not been started by any one hand. The roots of the movement seem to be the unused or undeveloped abilities of women and the conscientious belief of women, educators, and citizens that we are permitting a waste of ability that we cannot afford.

The first remarkable aspect of the conference is that its subject is taken so seriously that, at a time of year when academic pressures are very great, eighteen college presidents have attended, and the South, the East, the Middle West, and the Far West are all represented by leading educators. Many college and university deans of women and of men are also present, as are the leaders of many national organizations. The conversations have included the President of the National Council of Jewish Women, the President of the National Council of Negro Women, the Educational Director of the American Association of University Women, several members of the President's Commission on the Status of Women, the Assistant Secretary of Labor, representatives of great foundations, directors of workshops in vocations and human relations, and, most usefully, those who are presently in charge of pilot ventures in the continuing education of women.

The director of the American Personnel and Guidance Association was present, as was a representative of the International
Business Machines Corporation. This idea obviously has its
foot in some of the most important doors in the United States,
doors which are the entrances to a variety of modern thoughts
and actions.

If there ever was a conference without pride or pomposity,
it has been this one. Every paper which cited efforts in the field
of continuing education for women began with a statement about
the experimental nature of the work that was being done. None
boasted of a sure success. None had gathered enough case histories
and records to be assured or content. Instead of adding up
achievements, the leaders spoke of difficulties and resistances
which had to be overcome.

The conference began with a consideration of some of the
deepest and most subtle resistances. President O. Meredith Wilson,
both the host and the keynote speaker, threaded his talk with the
warning that a woman is a woman, saying, as did Dr. Karem M.
Monsour and President Gordon Blackwell, that women remain
an enigma to men. Although President Wilson said that "a
woman's need is differentiated from a man's need," when he
enumerated educational needs and possibilities, he also stated
that his words related to both men and women and that he would
make the same remarks to a committee of the legislature if he
were addressing them on educational matters. With that apparent
paradox, and President Wilson's statement that he was less interested in the plight of women than in the needs of society, the
major problems that were to concern the conference were laid
before it. They were recurrent. Most of what was said later, if
it was relevant to the discussion, was based on a consideration of
women's needs as differing from men's needs and on the fact that
the progress and education of men as well as women was inherent
in the development of continued and sustained education.

The brief period allowed for the meeting made it advisable to
have each session a plenary one, instead of dividing the group
into section meetings. This procedure not only gave the same
information to everyone but also made it possible to sense the
moods of the successive speakers. Each participant knew exactly

what had been said, where emphases had been laid, and the general reaction of the listeners. So the texture of this conference was more closely woven than is usually possible. The many suggestions made from the floor, plus all those reported from the breakfast meetings, add up to a very large body of working material which will be available for future development of projects.

The existence of resistance to the continuing education of women was presented early in the conference—and no one was allowed to forget it. Dr. Karem Monsour dealt with this in his discussion of the physical and psychological traits peculiar to women. He stated that unique aspects of a woman's life resist influence by culture, society, and education. He asserted that during certain periods in a woman's life—when she is in love, when she is bearing a child—it is impossible for her to learn. Disagreeing with his statement, Virginia Senders said that if there were such distracting periods of women's inability to learn, rethinking about women's entire education would be necessary. The conference was reminded by another commentator that men were also subject to emotional crises and often were not able to study when they were in love.

Dr. Monsour, in his paper and comments, indicated other resistances to continuing education for women. He suggested there might be male dominance at high levels of authority, perhaps disavowed or unconscious but nonetheless existent, and that there is resistance in the very educational processes that must be used by those who seek innovations. Some of his statements were hotly debated, but they were neither withdrawn by Dr. Monsour nor apparently rejected by the majority of his audience.

The subject of resistance to the education of women came up in several other talks and papers. There were contradictory findings. President C. Easton Rothwell of Mills College said that he had raised the question with a group of young mothers five to fifteen years out of college. They had just spent a year analyzing their own reactions to a questionnaire on continuing education of women and the job potential of a mother whose children are in school. These young women were almost unanimous and wholly unequivocal in their rejection of any return to work as an alternative to spending their full time as mothers. **On the** other hand, Mrs. Esther Peterson spoke of the study, *Fifteen Years After College: A Study of Alumnae of the Class of 1945,* completed by the Women's Bureau in which 580 alumnae of four colleges responded. A majority of these women felt the need of additional education or training to obtain the type of position they would like, and from 46 to 63 percent expressed interest in paid positions for the future.

The conflict in responses established little except the feeling among members of the conference that more research was necessary. It was obvious that in so large a picture one viewer might see one aspect and another quite a different one. Mrs. Peterson felt that women were "traditionally trapped" by marriage because their husbands' occupations kept them in one place. President Blackwell found, on the contrary, "our young people are among the most mobile group in the most mobile population of the world. The wife who married young and whose husband's work requires frequent moves often finds it necessary to study at several colleges before completing a degree."

Although these differences of opinion and observation cropped up in the conversations, agreements also emerged. No speaker questioned the value of counseling girls and women early in life and at later periods, too. The inadequacy of present counseling was referred to in almost every talk.

New directions began to be defined. President Rothwell believes that there will be new areas of activity for mature women— that even automation may be a useful factor. He advised the conference, "Look ahead for ten years and see what changes can be identified and verified." He suggested that we need "something a little harder and firmer on which to build."

No one doubted or denied the existence of impediments more definite than the built-in psychological ones. No one disputed that more money is needed to further the continuing education of women. Greater public interest is equally essential. Correlation of efforts to explain the reasons for continuing education of women and to promote the establishment and growth of plans and methods in this field is desirable.

There was general agreement that each university and college must select and develop a plan for the continuing education of women—and men—which is most suitable for the individual institution. The need for flexibility in the colleges and the serious problems of credits for the adult student and whether flexibility and innovation in proficiency examinations was possible in regard to them were spoken of many times. Modern methods of study by means of television, night courses, and programming for home study were endorsed. Donald McNeil, collaborator on the study, "The Role of the University in Adult Education," stated that most universities still paid only lip service to adult education and treated it with contempt. Surely, his criticism could not be applied to the participants in this conference.

Everyone who attended the conference possesses for study and reference the papers presented, and there is a stenographic record of the findings of the breakfast discussions. The mood of the meeting, its intention, its hesitations, and its vigor or enthusiasm are not in the reference book and cannot be taped, yet these are very important and, to some extent, can be summarized.

Examples of the differences between men and women, which undoubtedly create the need for a differentiation in their education, were seen again and again during the conference. These differences were evident in what Dr. Monsour spoke of as the "soft tongues" of the men when they talked to the women, in the deft compliments, in the flattering admissions that women were beyond understanding, in the affectionate references of husbands to wives and wives to husbands, and in the anecdotes of family life. We were men and women discussing the intricate problems of sex. In a way the conference proved its point: Women are different from men and are treated differently in many ways, including their education. Their education should be encouraged and improved, and it may be wiser to do it with "soft tongues" than with overardent demands. But it must be done, and it is being done.

The men and women who attended this conference will long remember the meeting on the second night when seven women told what is presently being done in pilot projects of continuing education for women. The case history of Lyda Boyer, with its vitality, adaptability, frankness, and unfinished quality, charmed everyone. It revealed a woman whose education surely will be continued.

Jane Berry of the University of Kansas told of the experiment under her direction and said that women who begin by taking noncredit courses often change and want to work for credit. Because there is such a variety of needs, she said, there must be a variety of plans.

Mrs. Helen Marston of Rutgers told of retraining for jobs which need the study of advanced mathematics. She did not forget to tell the audience that this retraining in mathematics increased a good family spirit and that children take pride in their mothers as students.

Mrs. Esther Raushenbush, director of continuing education at Sarah Lawrence College, explained the carefully selective work at that institution. Applicants must want to work toward a B.A. degree and have had at least a year of college before applying. She also spoke of the pleasure of counseling women whom Sarah Lawrence cannot accept and of advising them where to go for their special needs.

Constance Smith of the Institute for Independent Study at Radcliffe gave a picture of a different group—those to whom assistance is given for excellence in various intellectual fields. She said the presence of these very intelligent women who continue their education at Radcliffe raises the sights of the undergraduates.

Pauline Tompkins of the American Association of University Women outlined the objective of that organization's continuing education project, which is to provide teachers at the college level. A resource of mature, able, and available women exists, but if they are to become faculty members, their education must be subsidized. It is sometimes easier for a married woman supported by her husband to re-enter college life than it is for a single woman, who has the sole responsibility for earning her living. This creates another problem to be solved.

Finally, Vera Schletzer talked of the Minnesota Plan—its wide scope and its many clients. If there was no Minnesota Plan for the Continuing Education of Women, there would have been no conference at Itasca State Park. Full credit for the organization and management of the conference must go to Elizabeth Cless of the Minnesota Plan, who had almost full responsibility for its program and participants.

Five directors of plans for the continuing education of women attended this conference, but they are by no means the only directors of such plans. Margaret Habein Merry, chairman of the panel, had chaperoned this work from its inception and should be proud of the achievements that have come from an idea she had sponsored years ago. The pilot projects differ greatly. Their pattern is that they have no set pattern, but only a goal—happier and more useful women. As Esther Peterson remarked, if leisure implies uselessness, it is a sweet coating for a bitter pill.

Conference Participants

FLORENCE ANDERSON, Secretary of the Carnegie Corporation of New York and of the Carnegie Foundation for the Advancement of Teaching

MRS. MARGARET CULKIN BANNING, Author; Former Chairman, Commission on the Education of Women of the American Council on Education

LOUIS T. BENEZET, President, Colorado College

JANE BERRY, Director, University of Kansas City Project for Continuing Education of Women

GORDON W. BLACKWELL, President, Florida State University

MRS. ELLEN BODDY, Member, President's Commission on the Status of Women (Henrietta, Texas)

MRS. LYDA BOYER, Member of the Minnesota Plan for Continuing Education of Women

THOMAS CARROLL, President, George Washington University

MARTIN CHAMBERLAIN, Director, Continuing Education, University of Washington

ALEXANDER CHARTERS, Dean, University College, Syracuse University

MRS. ANTONIA CHAYES, Technical Secretary for the Committee on Education of the President's Commission on the Status of Women (Washington, D.C.)

SUSAN P. COBBS, Dean of the college, Swarthmore College

J. W. COHEN, Director, Inter-University Committee on the Superior Student (University of Colorado)

WILLIAM CONLEY, Director, Study of Catholic Education, University of Notre Dame

ALICE RICE COOK, Director, Human Relations Workshops, New School for Social Research

MARGARET CORMACK, Chairman of the Doctoral Program in Comparative and International Education, Department of Education, Brooklyn College

ANNE CRONIN, Director, Seven College Vocational Workshop (475 Riverside Drive, New York 27)

LAWRENCE E. DENNIS, Director, Commission on Academic Affairs, American Council on Education

MARY H. DONLON, Judge, United States Customs Court

SISTER MARY EDWARD, President, College of St. Catherine

MORTON GORDON, Associate Director, University Extension, University of California, Berkeley

CARL M. GRIP, Dean of Men, Temple University

MRS. EVA B. HANSL, Journalist and editor (New York City)

RUFUS C. HARRIS, President, Mercer University

DOROTHY HEIGHT, President, National Council of Negro Women

GRACE M. HENDERSON, Dean, College of Home Economics, Pennsylvania State University

MRS. MARGARET HICKEY, Public Affairs Editor, *Ladies Home Journal*

ARTHUR HITCHCOCK, Director, American Personnel and Guidance Association

MRS. MARJORIE HOWARD, Regent, University of Minnesota

MRS. VIOLA HYMES, President, National Council of Jewish Women

MRS. LOIS IRISH, Assistant Director, College Scholarship Service, College Entrance Examination Board

MARIANNA JENKINS, Associate Dean of the Woman's College, Duke University

MRS. PAULINE PARK WILSON KNAPP, President, Merrill-Palmer Institute (Michigan)

DOUGLAS M. KNIGHT, President, Lawrence College

HELEN LEBARON, Dean, College of Home Economics, Iowa State University

A. A. LIVERIGHT, Director, Center for the Study of Liberal Education for Adults (Illinois)

RITA MCCABE, Director of Planning Systems and Application Engineering, International Business Machines (New York City)

ERNEST E. MCMAHON, Dean, University College and the University Extension Division, Rutgers—The State University of New Jersey

DONALD MCNEIL, Collaborator in the study "The Role of the University in Adult Education" (Mesa, Arizona)

SISTER M. MADELEVA, C.S.C., Consultant to the President of St. Mary's College (Indiana)

MRS. HELEN M. MARSTON, Director, Retraining in Mathematics Program, University College, Rutgers—The State University of New Jersey

MARGARET J. MEALEY, Executive Director, National Council of Catholic Women

MRS. MARGARET HABEIN MERRY, Dean of Admissions, Radcliffe College

ROBERT MERRY, Director of the Doctoral Program, Graduate School of Business Administration, Harvard University

PAUL A. MILLER, President, West Virginia University

KAREM J. MONSOUR, M.D., Psychiatrist and psychoanalyst (Pasadena, California)

JAMES M. NABRIT, JR., President, Howard University

JOHN J. NEUMAIER, President, Moorhead State College

JULIUS M. NOLTE, Dean, General Extension Division, University of Minnesota

KATHRYN OLIPHANT, Consultant on Education, Association of the Junior Leagues of America, Inc.

MRS. ESTHER PETERSON, Assistant Secretary of Labor for Labor Standards and Director of the Women's Bureau, U.S. Department of Labor

ROYCE S. PITKIN, President, Goddard College

WILLA B. PLAYER, President, Bennett College

HARRY H. RANSOM, Chancellor, University of Texas

MRS. ESTHER RAUSHENBUSH, Director, Center for Continuing Education, Sarah Lawrence College

MARGUERITE RAWALT, Attorney (Washington, D.C.)

SISTER MARIA RENATA, C.S.C., President, St. Mary's College (Indiana)

CATHERINE J. ROBBINS, President, Pasadena City College

MRS. EUNICE E. ROBERTS, Assistant Dean for Undergraduate Development for Women's Educational Programs, Indiana University

NANCY G. ROMAN, Chief, Astronomy and Solar Physics Programs of the Office of Space Sciences, National Aeronautics and Space Administration

SISTER M. ROSALIE, Academic Dean, College of St. Catherine

C. EASTON ROTHWELL, President, Mills College

HELEN ROWAN, Editor, *Carnegie Quarterly*

BROTHER LEO V. RYAN, C.S.V., Director of Continuing Education, Marquette University

MRS. FELICE SCHWARTZ, Founder and President of "Catalyst"; Founder and First Executive Director, National Scholarship Service and Fund for Negro Students

MRS. VIRGINIA L. SENDERS, Consultant on Women's Education (Lincoln, Massachusetts)

GENE SETZER, Rockefeller Brothers Fund (New York City)

ALAN SIMPSON, Dean of the College, University of Chicago

CONSTANCE SMITH, Director, Radcliffe Institute for Independent Study

SEYMOUR A. SMITH, President, Stephens College

ERWIN R. STEINBERG, Dean, Margaret Morrison Carnegie College, Carnegie Institute of Technology

BERNARD H. STERN, Associate Director, School of General Studies, Brooklyn College of the City University of New York

WILLARD L. THOMPSON, Assistant to the President, University of Minnesota

PAULINE TOMPKINS, General Director, American Association of University Women

MRS. RUTH HILL USEEM, Research Consultant, Department of Sociology and Anthropology, Michigan State University

RUA VAN HORN, Vocational Education Division of the Office of Education, U.S. Department of Health, Education, and Welfare

GEORGE WAGGONER, Dean of Arts and Sciences, University of Kansas

JEAN WALTON, Dean of Women, Pomona College

PAUL L. WARD, President, Sarah Lawrence College

CAROLINE WARE, Historian for Unesco (Vienna, Virginia)

MRS. CYNTHIA C. WEDEL, Assistant General Secretary for Program, National Council of Churches of Christ in the U.S.A.

MRS. ESTHER M. WESTERVELT, Department of Guidance and Student Personnel Administration, Teachers College, Columbia University

O. MEREDITH WILSON, President, University of Minnesota

STEPHEN J. WRIGHT, President, Fisk University

E. W. ZIEBARTH, Dean of Summer Sessions, University of Minnesota

AMERICAN COUNCIL ON EDUCATION
Logan Wilson, *President*

The American Council on Education, founded in 1918, is a *council* of educational organizations and institutions. Its purpose is to advance education and educational methods through comprehensive voluntary and cooperative action on the part of American educational associations, organizations, and institutions.